GRADE 4 MATH BOOK

AMERICAN MATH ACADEMY

By H. TONG, M.Ed.

Math Instructor & Olympiad Coach

www.americanmathacademy.com

AMERICAN MATH
ACADEMY
GRADE 4
MATH BOOK

Writer: H.Tong
Copyright © 2023 The American Math Academy LLC.

All rights reserved. No part of this publication may be reproduced in whole or in part, stored in a retrieval system, or transmitted in any form or by any means electronic, mechanical, photocopying, recording or otherwise, without written permission of the copyright owner.

Printed in United States of America.

ISBN: 9798868473678

Although the writer has made every effort to ensure the accuracy and completeness of information contained this book, the writer assumes no responsibility for errors, inaccuracies, omissions or any inconsistency herein. Any slighting of people, places, or organizations is unintentional.

Questions, suggestions or comments, please email:americanmathacademy@gmail.com

TABLE OF CONTENTS

TABLE OF CONTENTS

TABLE OF CONTENTS

BOOKS BY AMERICA MATH ACADEMY

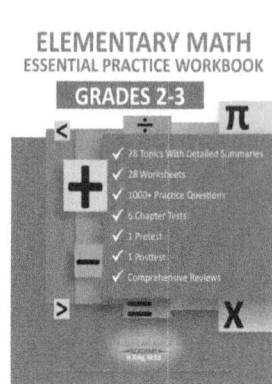

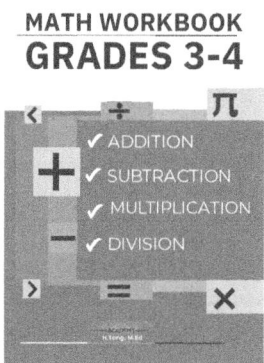

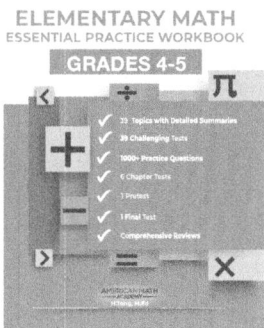

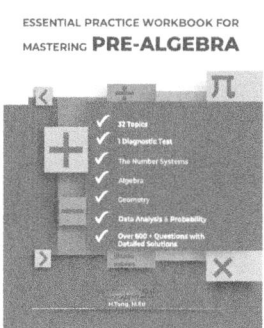

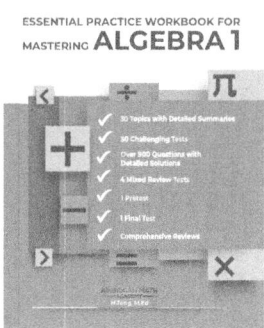

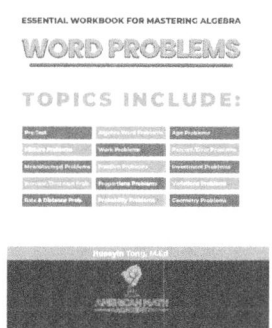

Kindergarten MATH WORKBOOK
From Zero to Math Hero

From Zero to Math Hero
Second Grade Math Mastery
GRADE 2 MATH BOOK
- 2,500+ Questions with Answers
- Covers all essential second grade math topics
From Beginner to Mastery Level

ELEMENTARY MATH
ESSENTIAL PRACTICE WORKBOOK
GRADES 2-3

From Zero to Math Hero
Third Grade Math Mastery
GRADE 3 MATH BOOK
- 2,500+ Questions with Answers
- Covers all essential third grade math topics
From Beginner to Mastery Level

MATH WORKBOOK
GRADES 3-4
- ADDITION
- SUBTRACTION
- MULTIPLICATION
- DIVISION

From Zero to Math Hero
Third Grade Math Mastery
GRADE 4 MATH BOOK
- 2,500+ Questions with Answers
- Covers all essential fourth grade math topics
From Beginner to Mastery Level

ELEMENTARY MATH
ESSENTIAL PRACTICE WORKBOOK
GRADES 4-5

ESSENTIAL PRACTICE WORKBOOK FOR
MASTERING **PRE-ALGEBRA**

THE COMPLETE GUIDE TO
MIDDLE SCHOOL MATH
GRADES 6-8
2ND EDITION

ESSENTIAL PRACTICE WORKBOOK FOR
MASTERING **ALGEBRA 1**

ALGEBRA II
ESSENTIAL PRACTICE WORKBOOK
HIGH SCHOOL

ESSENTIAL WORKBOOK FOR MASTERING ALGEBRA
WORD PROBLEMS
TOPICS INCLUDE:

BOOKS BY AMERICA MATH ACADEMY

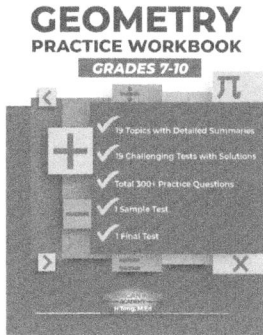

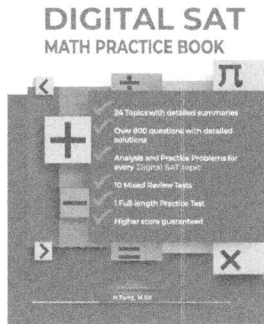

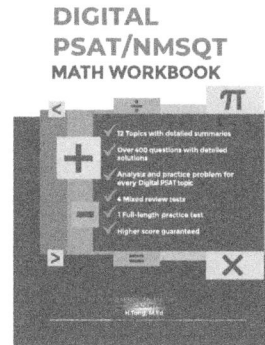

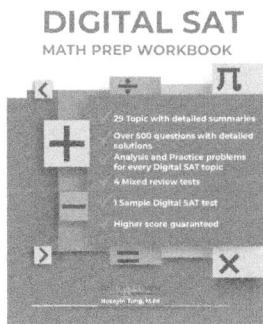

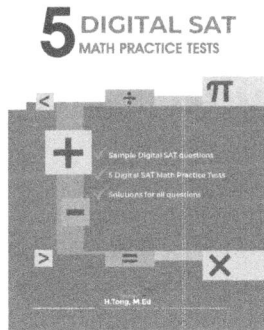

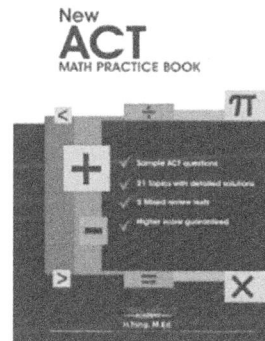

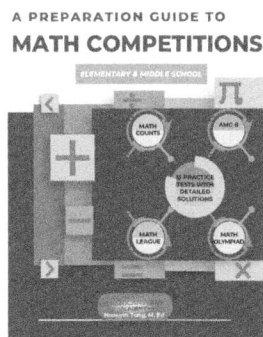

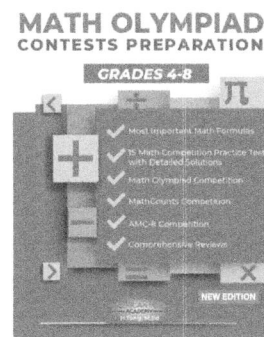

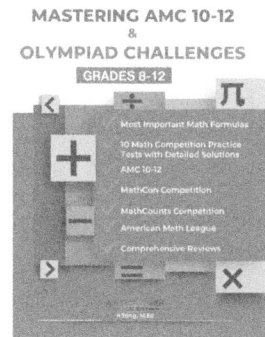

GEOMETRY
PRACTICE WORKBOOK
GRADES 7-10

- 19 Topics with Detailed Summaries
- 15 Challenging Tests with Solutions
- Total 300+ Practice Questions
- 1 Sample Test
- 1 Final Test

H.Tong, M.Ed

DIGITAL SAT
MATH PRACTICE BOOK

- 26 Topics with detailed summaries
- Over 800 questions with detailed solutions
- Analysis and Practice Problems for every Digital SAT topic
- 10 Mixed Review Tests
- 1 Full-length Practice Test
- Higher score guaranteed

H.Tong, M.Ed

DIGITAL PSAT/NMSQT
MATH WORKBOOK

- 12 Topics with detailed summaries
- Over 400 questions with detailed solutions
- Analysis and practice problem for every PSAT topic
- 4 Mixed review tests
- 1 Full-length practice test
- Higher score guaranteed

H.Tong, M.Ed

DIGITAL SAT
MATH PREP WORKBOOK

- 29 Topic with detailed summaries
- Over 800 questions with detailed solutions
- Analysis and Practice problems for every Digital SAT topic
- 4 Mixed review tests
- 1 Sample Digital SAT test
- Higher score guaranteed

Hosayn Tong, M.Ed

5 DIGITAL SAT
MATH PRACTICE TESTS

- Sample Digital SAT questions
- 5 Digital SAT Math Practice Tests
- Solutions for all questions

H.Tong, M.Ed

New ACT
MATH PRACTICE BOOK

- Sample ACT questions
- 21 Topics with detailed solutions
- 5 Mixed review tests
- Higher score guaranteed

H.Tong, M.Ed

A PREPARATION GUIDE TO
MATH COMPETITIONS
ELEMENTARY & MIDDLE SCHOOLS

- MATH COUNTS
- AMC 8
- 12 PRACTICE TESTS WITH DETAILED SOLUTIONS
- MATH LEAGUE
- MATH OLYMPIAD

Hosayn Tong, M. Ed

MATH OLYMPIAD
CONTESTS PREPARATION
GRADES 4-8

- Most Important Math Formulas
- 15 Math Competition Practice Tests with Detailed Solutions
- Math Olympiad Competition
- MathCounts Competition
- AMC-8 Competition
- Comprehensive Reviews

NEW EDITION

H.Tong, M.Ed

MASTERING AMC 10-12
& OLYMPIAD CHALLENGES
GRADES 8-12

- Most Important Math Formulas
- 10 Math Competition Practice Tests with Detailed Solutions
- AMC 10-12
- MathCon Competition
- MathCounts Competition
- American Math League
- Comprehensive Reviews

H.Tong, M.Ed

About the Author

Mr. Tong teaches at various private and public schools in both New York and New Jersey. In conjunction with his teaching, Mr. Tong developed his own private tutoring company. His company developed a unique way of ensuring their students' success on the math section of the SAT. His students, over the years, have been able to apply the knowledge and skills they learned during their tutoring sessions in college and beyond. Mr. Tong's academic accolades make him the best candidate to teach SAT Math. He received his master's degree in Math Education. He has won several national and state championships in various math competitions and has taken his team to victory in the Olympiads. He has trained students for Math Counts, American Math Competition (AMC), Harvard MIT Math Tournament, Princeton Math Contest, and the National Math League, and many other events. His teaching style ensures his students success. He personally invests energy and time into his students and sees what each individual struggles with. His dedication towards his students is evident through his student's achievements.

Acknowledgements

I would like to take the time to acknowledge the help and support of my beloved wife, my colleagues, and their feedback on my book was invaluable. Without everyone's help, this book would not be the same. I dedicate this book to my precious daughters Vera and Nora who were my inspiration to take on this project.

PRETEST

1) Find the quotient.

$5\overline{)368}$

A) 73R1

B) 73

C) 73R3

D) 141R3

2) Round to nearest ten.

943

A) 900

B) 940

C) 950

D) 960

3) What decimal is shown by the shaded part of this model?

A) 0.06

B) 0.6

C) 6

D) 60

4) What is the missing number on the number line?

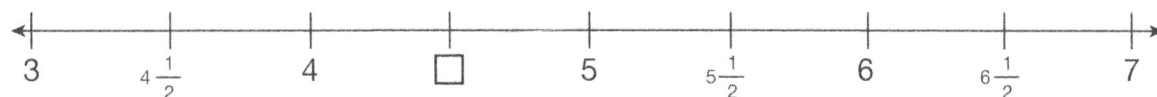

A) $3\dfrac{1}{2}$　　　C) $5\dfrac{1}{2}$

B) $4\dfrac{1}{2}$　　　D) $6\dfrac{1}{2}$

5) Which coordinate grid shows the ordered pair (4,3)?

A)

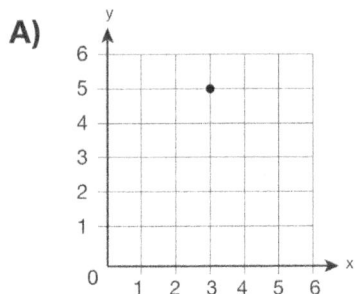

B)

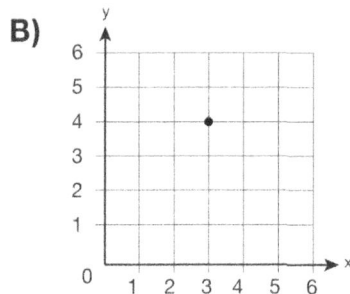

C)

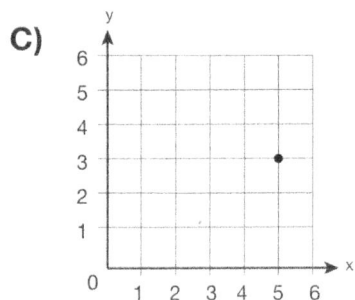

D)

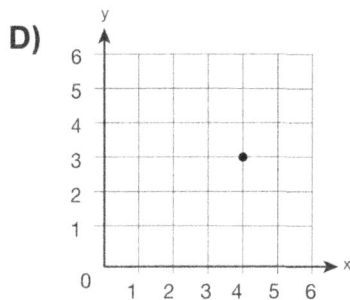

6) Nora has $75.00. She earns $21.00 more. How much money does Nora have in all?

A) $ 54

B) $ 88

C) $ 96

D) $ 106

7) Use the number line below to answer the question.

Which point is located at $11\frac{1}{4}$

A)   point X

B)   point Y

C)   point Z

D)   point N

PRETEST

8) Vera draws a shape on her paper. The shape has three sides. It has no pair of parallel sides. What shape does Vera draw?

A) Parallelogram

B) Rectangle

C) Square

D) Triangle

9) Which circle has $\dfrac{3}{4}$ shaded?

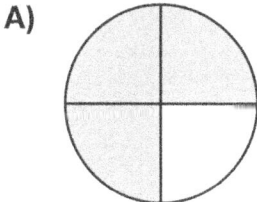

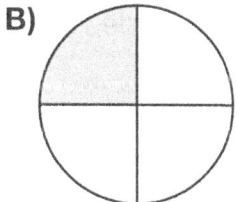

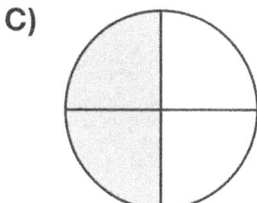

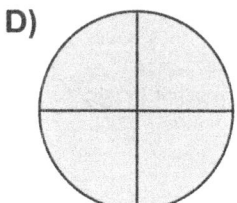

A)

B)

C)

D)

10) What letter names the point location by (2,2)?

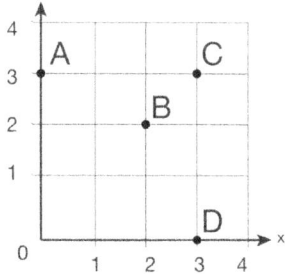

A) A   **B)** B   **C)** C   **D)** D

11) Use the picture below to answer the questions

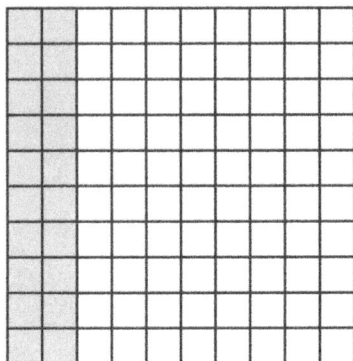

Which decimal number names the shaded part of this square?

A) 0.08

B) 0.20

C) 0.35

D) 0.48

12) Which letter has a pair of parallel lines?

A) X

B) L

C) H

D) T

13) Which number correctly completes the number sectence 90 x 44 = ___?

A) 360

B) 680

C) 2,960

D) 3,960

PRETEST

14) Use the table below to answer the question.

City	Population
A	24,350
B	24,050
C	28,315
D	28,350

Which list of city populations is in order from least to greatest?

A) 24,350;   24,050;   28,315;   28,350

B) 24,050;   24,350;   28,315;   20,350

C) 24,050;   24,350;   28,350;   28,315

D) 24,350;   28,350;   24,050;   28,315

15) Wich number correctly completes the subtraction sentence 4 - 2.15 = ___?

A) 1.35

B) 1.55

C) 1.65

D) 1.85

16) Find the quotient.

4)645

A) 161

B) 161 R1

C) 162

D) 165

17) Use the table below to answer the question.

Sport	Number of Votes
A	10
B	5
C	7
D	2

The students in the fifth grade class voted for their favorite sport. Which bar graph shows results of the students vote?

A)

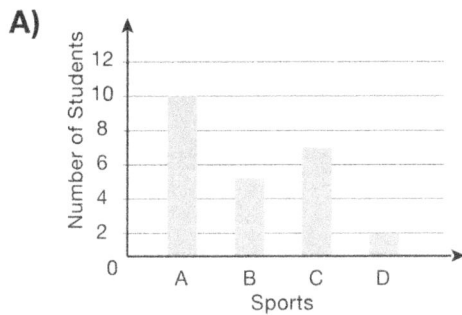

B)

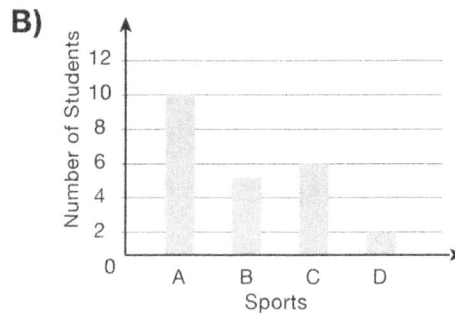

C)

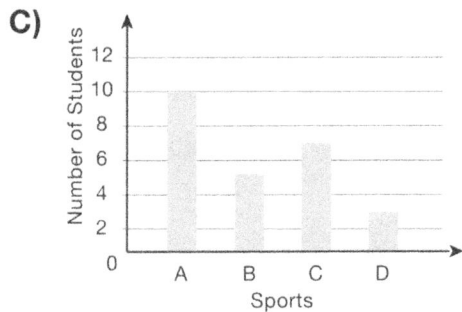

D)

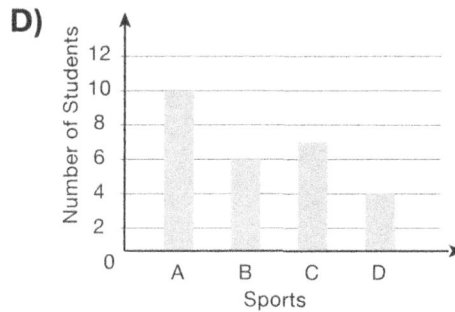

18) Round 148 to the nearest ten.

A) 100   **B)** 140   **C)** 150   **D)** 200

19) Solve.

45 x 100 = ___

A) 45   **B)** 450   **C)** 4,500   **D)** 45,000

PRETEST

20) Which triangle has one right angle?

A)

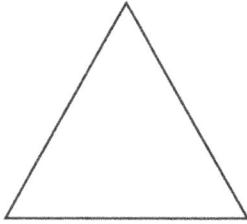

B)

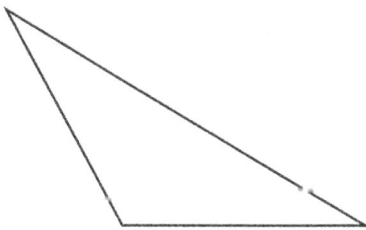

C)

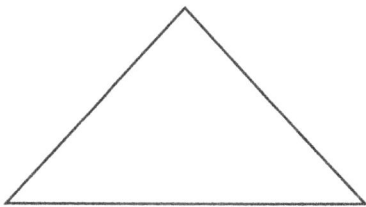

D)

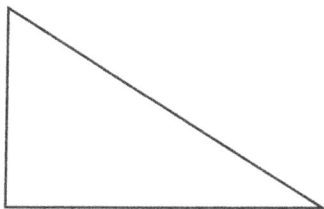

21) A building is 48 feet high. What is the height of the building in yards?

A)   1 yards

B)   4 yards

C)   8 yards

D)   16 yards

PLACE VALUE

Place Value Chart

Millions	Hundred Thousands	Ten Thousands	Thousands	Hundreds	Tens	Ones	Decimal Point	Tenths	Hundredths	Thousandths
1	3	5	6	7	8	9	●	7	6	4

Whole Numbers | Decimal Numbers

One million, three hundred fifty six thousand, seven hundred eighty nine and 7 hundred sixty four thousandths

Expanded Form

Example: Write **35,678** in **expanded form.**

Solution:

35,678: (3 x 10,000) + (5 x 1,000) + (6 x 100) + (7 x 10) + (8 x 1)

= 30,000 + 5,000 + 600 + 70 + 8

Standard Form

Example: Write Eight million, nine thousand four hundred fifty-six in **standard form**

Solution: 8,009,456

Word Form

Example: Write 6,767 in **word form.**

Solution:

6,767: Six thousand and seven hundred sixty-seven.

WORKSHEET 1

Write each of following number in expanded form.

1) 9,234,456: _____

_____

2) 7,891,345: _____

_____

3) 845,612: _____

_____

4) 56,231: _____

_____

5) 6,917: _____

_____

6) 291: _____

_____

7) 31: _____

_____

8) 56,200: _____

_____

9) 6,901: _____

_____

10) 50,836: _____

_____

Standard Form

Write each of following number in **standard form.**

1) $(6 \times 1,000,000) + (7 \times 100,000) + (8 \times 10,000) + (9 \times 1000) + (9 \times 100) + (1 \times 10) + (4 \times 1)$

_____

2) $(6 \times 100,000) + (6 \times 10,000) + (7 \times 1,000) + (9 \times 100) + (5 \times 10) + (2 \times 1)$

_____

3) $(9 \times 1,000,000) + (6 \times 100,000) + (9 \times 10,000) + (8 \times 1,000) + (7 \times 100) + (3 \times 10) + (4 \times 1)$

_____

4) $(8 \times 10,000) + (7 \times 1,000) + (9 \times 100) + (5 \times 10) + (3 \times 1)$

_____

5) $(9 \times 1000) + (4 \times 100) + (9 \times 10) + (8 \times 1)$

_____

6) $(5 \times 10,000,000) + (6 \times 1,000,000) + (4 \times 100,000) + (8 \times 10,000) + (2 \times 1,000)$
$+ (3 \times 100) + (4 \times 10) + (5 \times 1)$

_____

7) $(9 \times 1,000,000) + (6 \times 100,000) + (9 \times 10,000) + (8 \times 1,000) + (7 \times 100) + (3 \times 10) + (4 \times 1)$

_____

8) Four thousand and six hundred fourty three

_____

9) Nine hundred nineteen

_____

10) Eight thousand and four hundred sixty five

_____

11) Four hundred sixty one

_____

AMERICAN MATH
ACADEMY

WORKSHEET 3

Write each of following number in **word form.**

1) 7,735,645: _____

_____

2) 785,125: _____

_____

3) 35,578: _____

_____

4) 5,974: _____

_____

5) 678: _____

_____

6) 3,000 + 300 + 30 + 3

_____

7) 4,000 + 400 + 20 + 9

_____

8) 60,000 + 7,000 + 100 + 90 + 2

_____

9) (3 × 100,000) + (6 × 10,000) + (7 × 1,000) + (5 × 100) + (7 × 10) + (4 × 1)

_____

10) (3 × 1,000) + (6 × 100) + (4 × 10) + (9 × 1)

_____

Comparing Numbers

WORKSHEET 4

Compering Numbers

Example: Which number is greater, 3,567 or 3,547?

Solution:

$\left.\begin{array}{l} 3{,}567 \\ 3{,}547 \end{array}\right\rangle$ Line up the digits.

$\left.\begin{array}{l} 3{,}5\underline{6}7 \\ 3{,}5\underline{4}7 \end{array}\right\rangle$ Compare the digits that are different.

Since, 6 is greater than 4. So, 3,567 is greater than 3,547.

3,567 > 3,547

Compare each of following pair of numbers. Write >, < or = for each.

1)   645 ◯ 655   2)   1,567 ◯ 1,577

3)   58 ◯ 57   4)   105 ◯ 115

5)   1,996 ◯ 1,896   6)   2,021 ◯ 2,202

7)   1,899 ◯ 1,896   8)   3,200 ◯ 3,202

9)   3,850 ◯ 3,870   10)   5,204 ◯ 5,304

11)   2,2035 ◯ 2,2035   12)   2,026 ◯ 2,026

13)   200,203 ◯ 200,204   14)   2,220 ◯ 2,201

15)   2,203 ◯ 2,204   16)   2,210 ◯ 2,215

17)   2,403 ◯ 2,504   18)   2,980 ◯ 2,890

AMERICAN MATH
ACADEMY

WORKSHEET 5

Write the numbers in order from least to greatest.

1) 165   325   986   _____   _____   _____

2) 13,520   8,962   7,778   _____   _____   _____

3) 750   650   365   _____   _____   _____

4) 6,666   5,555   4,444   _____   _____   _____

5) 12,350   4,980   7,456   _____   _____   _____

6) 13,500   13,450   13,300   _____   _____   _____

7) 11,380   15,490   11,470   _____   _____   _____

8) 16,792   16,795   16,770   _____   _____   _____

9) 20,154   20,054   18,950   _____   _____   _____

10) 968   10,750   9,875   _____   _____   _____

11) 3,678   7,765   15,384   _____   _____   _____

12) 9,128   12,368   77,998   _____   _____   _____

13) 10,166   10,186   10,161   _____   _____   _____

14) 5,486   5,488   5,468   _____   _____   _____

Rounding Numbers

- Identify the units digit
- Round up or down
- If the digit is 5 or greater, add one more.
- If the digit is less than 5, leave it the same.

Example: Round 68 to the nearest tens.

Solution:

Keep the 6.

The next digit is "8" which is 5 or more, so increase the "6" by 1 to 7. The answer is 70.

Round each number to the place value of the underlined digit.

1) 6,780,089   **2)** 34,678,457

3) 503,132   **4)** 7,184

5) 2,345,678   **6)** 375

Round each number to the place value indicated.

7) 456,346; hundreds   **8)** 1,234; tens

9) 3,547,892; thousands   **10)** 12,345,756; millions

11) 125; ones   **12)** 68; ones

13) 789; tens   **14)** 894; tens

15) 1,364; hundreds   **16)** 697,365; tens

17) 3,389; ones   **18)** 12,965; hundreds

WORKSHEET 7

Round each number to the nearest thousand.

1) 3,350 _____ 2) 7,665 _____ 3) 4,850 _____

4) 8,945 _____ 5) 7,965 _____ 6) 12,825 _____

7) 12,350 _____ 8) 18,495 _____ 9) 16,872 _____

10) 22,398 _____ 11) 25,396 _____ 12) 13,983 _____

Round each number to the nearest ten thousand.

13) 22,300 _____ 14) 17,375 _____ 15) 76,384 _____

16) 78,960 _____ 17) 120,690 _____ 18) 16,564 _____

19) 495,398 _____ 20) 39,870 _____ 21) 73,690 _____

22) 186,376 _____ 23) 67,946 _____ 24) 79,642 _____

Addition

WORKSHEET 8

Adding Numbers

- Line up the numbers and fill in any empty places with zeros, then add the whole numbers

Example: add 3,456 + 4,342

Solution:
$$\begin{array}{r} 3,456 \\ 4,342 \\ + \hline \\ 7,798 \end{array}$$

For questions 1 through 27, add.

1) 6,356 + 5,302 = _____

2) 1,734 + 2,987 = _____

3) 3,698 + 2,125 = _____

4) 12,345 + 10,302 = _____

5) 123,734 + 204,987 = _____

6) 7,390 + 6,350 = _____

7) 13,000 + 5,200 = _____

8) 123,567 + 2,900 = _____

9) 12,350 + 15,750 = _____

10) 125 + 3,567 = _____

11) 1,205 + 2,905 = _____

12) 10,390 + 11,250 = _____

13) 14,567 + 205 = _____

14) 1,879 + 2,050 = _____

15) 6,780 + 13,750 = _____

16)
$$\begin{array}{r} 1,678 \\ 1,405 \\ + \hline \end{array}$$

17)
$$\begin{array}{r} 7,645 \\ 10,208 \\ + \hline \end{array}$$

18)
$$\begin{array}{r} 7,665 \\ 3,912 \\ + \hline \end{array}$$

19)
$$\begin{array}{r} 12,983 \\ 13,404 \\ + \hline \end{array}$$

20)
$$\begin{array}{r} 123,809 \\ 204,208 \\ + \hline \end{array}$$

21)
$$\begin{array}{r} 6,390 \\ 7,450 \\ + \hline \end{array}$$

22)
$$\begin{array}{r} 105,987 \\ 210,400 \\ + \hline \end{array}$$

23)
$$\begin{array}{r} 678,806 \\ 567,208 \\ + \hline \end{array}$$

24)
$$\begin{array}{r} 48,390 \\ 52,185 \\ + \hline \end{array}$$

25)
$$\begin{array}{r} 985,000 \\ 134,492 \\ + \hline \end{array}$$

26)
$$\begin{array}{r} 1,677,805 \\ 127,203 \\ + \hline \end{array}$$

27)
$$\begin{array}{r} 128,396 \\ 258,597 \\ + \hline \end{array}$$

AMERICAN MATH
—ACADEMY—

WORKSHEET 9

Add.

1)   16,395
      18,456
+ _____

2)   73,690
      75,985
+ _____

3)   39,498
      18,750
+ _____

4)   16,350
      25,490
+ _____

5)   61,250
      71,350
+ _____

6)   125,390
      250,125
+ _____

7)   186,498
      167,666
+ _____

8)   409,760
      360,784
+ _____

9)   666,798
      333,765
+ _____

10)   965,125
      118,667
+ _____

11)   999,676
      365,400
+ _____

12)   176,394
      548,676
+ _____

13)   196,356
      185,465
+ _____

14)   18,350
      19,250
+ _____

15)   125,698
      148,356
+ _____

Subtraction

Subtracting Numbers

- Line up the numbers and fill in any empty places with zeros, then subtract the whole numbers.

Example: Subtract 225 – 134

Solution:
$$\begin{array}{r} \overset{\scriptstyle 112}{2\cancel{2}5} \\ -\ 134 \\ \hline 91 \end{array}$$

For questions 1 through 27, subtract.

1) 6,353 – 5,402 = _____

2) 1,836 – 1,582 = _____

3) 6,350 – 2,125 = _____

4) 12,345 – 10,302 = _____

5) 123,734 – 112,987 = _____

6) 19,350 – 12,125 = _____

7) 13,000 – 5,200 = _____

8) 6,567 – 1,900 = _____

9) 4,958 – 3,256 = _____

10) 9,125 – 3,567 = _____

11) 1,995 – 1,905 = _____

12) 11,369 – 10,765 = _____

13) 14,567 – 205 = _____

14) 1,879 – 1,050 = _____

15) 22,198 – 17,666 = _____

16)
$$\begin{array}{r} 1,678 \\ -\ 1,405 \\ \hline \end{array}$$

17)
$$\begin{array}{r} 7,645 \\ -\ 6,208 \\ \hline \end{array}$$

18)
$$\begin{array}{r} 13,540 \\ -\ 12,450 \\ \hline \end{array}$$

19)
$$\begin{array}{r} 12,983 \\ -\ 11,404 \\ \hline \end{array}$$

20)
$$\begin{array}{r} 123,809 \\ -\ 104,208 \\ \hline \end{array}$$

21)
$$\begin{array}{r} 125,698 \\ -\ 104,125 \\ \hline \end{array}$$

22)
$$\begin{array}{r} 125,987 \\ -\ 110,400 \\ \hline \end{array}$$

23)
$$\begin{array}{r} 678,806 \\ -\ 567,208 \\ \hline \end{array}$$

24)
$$\begin{array}{r} 13,960 \\ -\ 12,980 \\ \hline \end{array}$$

25)
$$\begin{array}{r} 985,000 \\ -\ 134,492 \\ \hline \end{array}$$

26)
$$\begin{array}{r} 1,677,805 \\ -\ 127,203 \\ \hline \end{array}$$

27)
$$\begin{array}{r} 29,946 \\ -\ 28,350 \\ \hline \end{array}$$

WORKSHEET 11

Subtract.

1)   12,350
      10,420
-

2)   9,280
      8,450
-

3)   5,390
      4,280
-

4)   13,965
      11,195
-

5)   16,960
      14,380
-

6)   17,965
      13,795
-

7)   73,650
      48,490
-

8)   77,960
      51,660
-

9)   72,960
      14,999
-

10)   71,390
      39,490
-

11)   66,666
      43,996
-

12)   7,777
      6,969
-

13)   444,765
      333,948
-

14)   186,791
      184,965
-

15)   151,250
      146,310
-

Addition and Subtraction

Add or subtract.

1) 18,496
    12,548
+ _____

2) 13,698
    12,795
- _____

3) 36,978
    17,665
+ _____

4) 13,697
    11,798
- _____

5) 126,666
    142,777
+ _____

6) 19,668
    12,725
- _____

7) 16,570
    18,790
+ _____

8) 66,742
    77,354
+ _____

9) 128,640
    120,742
- _____

10) 19,756
    20,390
+ _____

11) 148,350
    121,390
- _____

12) 667,742
    721,498
+ _____

13) 161,390
    141,280
- _____

14) 18,378
    11,221
+ _____

15) 263,742
    122,341
- _____

WORKSHEET 13

Multiply.

1) 6 x 7 =____   2) 8 x 9 =____   3) 12 x 8 =____   4) 20 x 3 =____

5) 10 x 8 =____   6) 12 x 6 =____   7) 15 x 3 =____   8) 18 x 5 =____

9) 18 x 4 =____   10) 18 x 7 =____   11) 12 x 9 =____   12) 16 x 3 =____

13) 13 x 7 =____   14) 15 x 9 =____   15) 9 x 14 =____   16) 20 x 4 =____

17) 6 x 15 =____   18) 8 x 13 =____   19) 9 x 17 =____   20) 7 x 17 =____

21) 17 x 5 =____   22) 18 x 6 =____   23) 13 x 4 =____   24) 11 x 9 =____

25) 11 x 4 =____   26) 18 x 6 =____   27) 15 x 5 =____   28) 4 x 17 =____

WORKSHEET 14

Multiply.

1) 2 x _____ = 48   **2)** 9 x _____ = 81   **3)** _____ x 8 = 80   **4)** 2 x _____ = 42

5) _____ x 16 = 32   **6)** 8 x _____ = 64   **7)** _____ x 4 = 12   **8)** 10 x _____ = 100

9) 10 x _____ = 90   **10)** _____ x 24 = 96   **11)** 10 x _____ = 70   **12)** 8 x _____ = 0

13) 12 x _____ = 36   **14)** 4 x _____ = 0   **15)** _____ x 7 = 56   **16)** _____ x 7 = 42

17) 5 x _____ = 35   **18)** _____ x 8 = 48   **19)** _____ x 3 = 45   **20)** _____ x 8 = 88

21) _____ x 9 = 72   **22)** _____ x 8 = 56   **23)** 7 x _____ = 63   **24)** 6 x _____ = 72

25) _____ x 11 = 99   **26)** _____ x 4 = 40   **27)** _____ x 10 = 0   **28)** 3 x _____ = 27

AMERICAN MATH
— ACADEMY —

WORKSHEET 15

Write the missing numbers.

1)

_____ rows of _____ = _____

_____ x _____ = _____

2)

_____ rows of _____ = _____

_____ x _____ = _____

3)

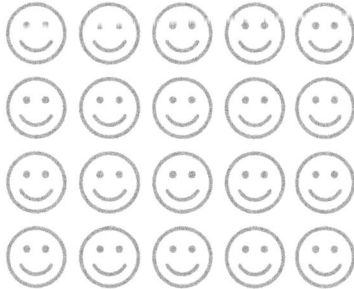

_____ rows of _____ = _____

_____ x _____ = _____

4)

_____ rows of _____ = _____

_____ x _____ = _____

5)

_____ rows of _____ = _____

_____ x _____ = _____

6)

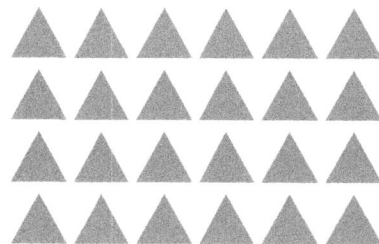

_____ rows of _____ = _____

_____ x _____ = _____

Estimating Products

Estimate by rounding the second factor to the nearest ten.

1) 6 x 19   is   6 x **20** = **120**

2) 8 x 48   is   8 x _____ = _____

3) 6 x 69   is   6 x _____ = _____

4) 7 x 43   is   7 x _____ = _____

5) 5 x 68   is   5 x _____ = _____

6) 4 x 99   is   4 x _____ = _____

7) 3 x 37   is   3 x _____ = _____

8) 2 x 99   is   2 x _____ = _____

9) 9 x 47   is   9 x _____ = _____

10) 8 x 63   is   8 x _____ = _____

WORKSHEET 17

Example: $6 \times 45 = 6(40 + 5) = (6 \times 40) + (6 \times 5) =$
$$= 240 + 30 = 270$$

Fill in the blanks.

1) $6 \times 78 = 6 \times (\underline{\hspace{1cm}} + \underline{\hspace{1cm}})$

   $6 \times 78 = (6 \times \underline{\hspace{1cm}}) + (6 \times \underline{\hspace{1cm}})$

   $6 \times 78 = \underline{\hspace{1cm}} + \underline{\hspace{1cm}}$

   $6 \times 78 = \underline{\hspace{1cm}}$

2) $9 \times 27 = 9 \times (\underline{\hspace{1cm}} + \underline{\hspace{1cm}})$

   $9 \times 27 = (9 \times \underline{\hspace{1cm}}) + (9 \times \underline{\hspace{1cm}})$

   $9 \times 27 = \underline{\hspace{1cm}} + \underline{\hspace{1cm}}$

   $9 \times 27 = \underline{\hspace{1cm}}$

3) $8 \times 79 = 8 \times (\underline{\hspace{1cm}} + \underline{\hspace{1cm}})$

   $8 \times 79 = (8 \times \underline{\hspace{1cm}}) + (8 \times \underline{\hspace{1cm}})$

   $8 \times 79 = \underline{\hspace{1cm}} + \underline{\hspace{1cm}}$

   $8 \times 79 = \underline{\hspace{1cm}}$

One-Digit by Two-Digit Multiplication

WORKSHEET 18

Multiply.

1) $\begin{array}{r} 18 \\ \times\ 3 \\ \hline \end{array}$	**2)** $\begin{array}{r} 16 \\ \times\ 4 \\ \hline \end{array}$	**3)** $\begin{array}{r} 25 \\ \times\ 8 \\ \hline \end{array}$	**4)** $\begin{array}{r} 65 \\ \times\ 2 \\ \hline \end{array}$
5) $\begin{array}{r} 12 \\ \times\ 5 \\ \hline \end{array}$	**6)** $\begin{array}{r} 84 \\ \times\ 3 \\ \hline \end{array}$	**7)** $\begin{array}{r} 68 \\ \times\ 3 \\ \hline \end{array}$	**8)** $\begin{array}{r} 13 \\ \times\ 9 \\ \hline \end{array}$
9) $\begin{array}{r} 74 \\ \times\ 5 \\ \hline \end{array}$	**10)** $\begin{array}{r} 78 \\ \times\ 6 \\ \hline \end{array}$	**11)** $\begin{array}{r} 64 \\ \times\ 8 \\ \hline \end{array}$	**12)** $\begin{array}{r} 69 \\ \times\ 3 \\ \hline \end{array}$
13) $\begin{array}{r} 71 \\ \times\ 8 \\ \hline \end{array}$	**14)** $\begin{array}{r} 18 \\ \times\ 8 \\ \hline \end{array}$	**15)** $\begin{array}{r} 71 \\ \times\ 4 \\ \hline \end{array}$	**16)** $\begin{array}{r} 73 \\ \times\ 8 \\ \hline \end{array}$
17) $\begin{array}{r} 64 \\ \times\ 6 \\ \hline \end{array}$	**18)** $\begin{array}{r} 72 \\ \times\ 8 \\ \hline \end{array}$	**19)** $\begin{array}{r} 88 \\ \times\ 5 \\ \hline \end{array}$	**20)** $\begin{array}{r} 90 \\ \times\ 6 \\ \hline \end{array}$
21) $\begin{array}{r} 19 \\ \times\ 8 \\ \hline \end{array}$	**22)** $\begin{array}{r} 15 \\ \times\ 7 \\ \hline \end{array}$	**23)** $\begin{array}{r} 75 \\ \times\ 4 \\ \hline \end{array}$	**24)** $\begin{array}{r} 98 \\ \times\ 6 \\ \hline \end{array}$

AMERICAN MATH
— ACADEMY —

WORKSHEET 19

Multiply.

1) 648 × 3	**2)** 142 × 9	**3)** 722 × 4	**4)** 642 × 5
5) 768 × 6	**6)** 768 × 4	**7)** 498 × 3	**8)** 382 × 6
9) 771 × 3	**10)** 392 × 9	**11)** 189 × 8	**12)** 366 × 6
13) 762 × 9	**14)** 456 × 2	**15)** 865 × 7	**16)** 912 × 6
17) 198 × 9	**18)** 365 × 5	**19)** 256 × 4	**20)** 728 × 3
21) 358 × 2	**22)** 499 × 4	**23)** 256 × 6	**24)** 421 × 7

Two-Digit by Two-Digit Multiplication

Example: 53 x 35 = ____   ⟶   53
                                    × 35
Note: • Line up the numbers.   255
       • Start multipling by ones digit then tens digit.   + 590
       • Add the product then regroup if needed.
                                    1,850

Multiply.

1)	66	2)	88	3)	75	4)	79	5)	81
	× 12		× 11		× 18		× 13		× 16

6)	99	7)	83	8)	89	9)	76	10)	79
	× 13		× 19		× 17		× 81		× 61

11)	18	12)	19	13)	65	14)	46	15)	69
	× 56		× 29		× 72		× 12		× 75

16)	66	17)	54	18)	48	19)	56	20)	75
	× 55		× 25		× 18		× 19		× 13

21)	68	22)	74	23)	98	24)	99	25)	84
	× 12		× 16		× 13		× 28		× 22

AMERICAN MATH
ACADEMY

WORKSHEET 21

Divide.

1) $18 \div 6 =$ _____

2) $33 \div 3 =$ _____

3) $18 \div 3 =$ _____

4) $42 \div 7 =$ _____

5) $66 \div 11 =$ _____

6) $24 \div 8 =$ _____

7) $64 \div 4 =$ _____

8) $25 \div 5 =$ _____

9) $48 \div 4 =$ _____

10) $56 \div 7 =$ _____

11) $80 \div 8 =$ _____

12) $42 \div 6 =$ _____

13) $70 \div 7 =$ _____

14) $26 \div 2 =$ _____

15) $24 \div 4 =$ _____

16) $50 \div 5 =$ _____

17) $63 \div 7 =$ _____

18) $72 \div 6 =$ _____

19) $36 \div 4 =$ _____

20) $84 \div 12 =$ _____

21) $99 \div 9 =$ _____

22) $88 \div 11 =$ _____

23) $66 \div 6 =$ _____

24) $72 \div 8 =$ _____

25) $16 \div 2 =$ _____

26) $72 \div 12 =$ _____

27) $49 \div 7 =$ _____

Long Division

Divide.

1) $8\overline{)88}$ 2) $6\overline{)72}$ 3) $3\overline{)51}$ 4) $3\overline{)66}$

5) $9\overline{)81}$ 6) $3\overline{)18}$ 7) $5\overline{)90}$ 8) $5\overline{)50}$

9) $8\overline{)82}$ 10) $2\overline{)68}$ 11) $2\overline{)74}$ 12) $4\overline{)68}$

13) $5\overline{)81}$ 14) $7\overline{)69}$ 15) $6\overline{)77}$ 16) $3\overline{)65}$

17) $8\overline{)77}$ 18) $7\overline{)99}$ 19) $9\overline{)48}$ 20) $6\overline{)98}$

21) $5\overline{)66}$ 22) $6\overline{)53}$ 23) $4\overline{)87}$ 24) $7\overline{)93}$

AMERICAN MATH
ACADEMY

WORKSHEET 23

Divide.

1)
```
      217
  4 ) 868
    - 8
      06
    -  4
      28
    - 28
       0
```

2) 5) 895

3) 3) 483

4) 4) 672

5) 4) 446

6) 3) 768

7) 2) 107

8) 3) 863

9) 6) 582

10) 8) 136

11) 9) 234

12) 4) 208

13) 5) 697

14) 5) 126

15) 7) 119

16) 2) 896

Factors

Factors are the numbers multiply together to get another numbers.

Factor of 20: __1__, __2__, __4__, __5__, __10__, __20__,   1 x 20 = 20, 2 x 10 = 20, 4 x 5 = 20

Write all of the factors of each numbers.

1) 48 : ____, ____, ____, ____, ____, ____, ____, ____, ____, ____,

2) 51 : ____, ____, ____, ____,

3) 19 : ____, ____,

4) 15 : ____, ____, ____, ____,

5) 30 : ____, ____, ____, ____, ____, ____, ____,

6) 65 : ____, ____, ____, ____,

7) 90 : ____, ____, ____, ____, ____, ____, ____, ____, ____, ____,

8) 77 : ____, ____, ____, ____,

9) 100 : ____, ____, ____, ____, ____, ____, ____, ____, ____,

10) 49 : ____, ____, ____,

11) 54 : ____, ____, ____, ____, ____, ____, ____, ____,

12) 39 : ____, ____, ____, ____,

WORKSHEET 25

Prime numbers: A number that has only two factors, 1 and itself.

Composite numbers: A number that has more than two factos.

Examples: 4, 6, 8, 10, ...

Note: 0 and 1 are netiher.

---

1) Circle the numbers from list that are prime numbers:

1	2	3	4	5
6	7	8	9	10
11	12	13	14	15
16	17	18	19	20
21	22	23	24	25

2) Circle the numbers from list that are composite numbers:

1	2	3	4	5
6	7	8	9	10
11	12	13	14	15
16	17	18	19	20
21	22	23	24	25

Adding and Subtracting Patterns

WORKSHEET 26

Example: Complete the patterns in each of following table.

1)

Add 10	3	6	9	12	15	18

2)

Add 15	12	22	32	42	52	62

3)

Subtract 5	5	10	15	20	25	30

4)

Subtract 6	6	12	24	36	48	60

5)

Add 12	9	18	27	36	45	54

6)

Add 20	1	3	5	7	9	11

7)

Subtract 8	10	20	30	40	50	60

8)

Subtract 10	20	35	45	55	65	75

9)

Add 10	10	23	35	47	59	61

10)

Add 20	32	37	42	47	52	57

AMERICAN MATH
ACADEMY

WORKSHEET 27

Example: Complete the patterns in each of following table.

1)

Multiply by 4	7	8	9	10	11

2)

Multiply by 5	12	13	14	15	16

3)

Multiply by 6	15	20	25	30	35

4)

Multiply by 7	6	12	18	24	36

5)

Divide by 11	11	33	44	55	66	77

6)

Divide by 10	10	30	50	70	90	100

7)

Multiply by 5	8	10	12	14	16	18

8)

Multiply by 3	11	13	15	17	19	21

9)

Divide by 2	24	36	48	54	60	66

10)

Divide by 7	14	21	28	35	49	63

Fractions and Types of Fractions

Fractions: Fractions are numbers that can be in the form $\frac{A}{B}$, where B is not equel by zero.

Examples: $\frac{1}{2}$, $\frac{1}{3}$, $\frac{2}{5}$, ... ($\frac{A}{B}$ $\longrightarrow$ Numerator $\longrightarrow$ Denominator)

Types of Fractions:

Proper Fractions: A fractions were the numerator is less than the denominator.

Examples: $\frac{1}{2}$, $\frac{3}{5}$, $\frac{4}{7}$, ...

Improper Fractions: A fraction were the denominator is less than the numerator.

Examples: $\frac{7}{3}$, $\frac{10}{9}$, $\frac{11}{3}$, ...

Mixed Fractions: When a fraction is written in the form $A\frac{B}{C}$

Examples: $1\frac{1}{2}$, $3\frac{1}{4}$, $7\frac{2}{5}$, ...

Identify whether the following fractions are proper or improper.

1) $\frac{1}{2}$

2) $\frac{4}{5}$

3) $\frac{1}{9}$

4) $\frac{13}{9}$

5) $\frac{25}{8}$

6) $\frac{9}{10}$

7) $\frac{131}{18}$

8) $\frac{145}{205}$

9) $\frac{19}{21}$

10) $\frac{25}{24}$

11) Which of following is a proper fraction?

A) $\frac{19}{18}$ B) $\frac{13}{12}$ C) $\frac{1}{18}$ D) $\frac{4}{3}$

12) Which of following is a mixed fraction?

A) $\frac{1}{6}$ B) $\frac{2}{3}$ C) $\frac{1}{5}$ D) $1\frac{1}{3}$

13) Which of following is an improper fraction?

A) $\frac{1}{8}$ B) $\frac{3}{4}$ C) $\frac{1}{2}$ D) $\frac{4}{3}$

14) $\frac{1}{3}$ is which of following type of fraction?

A) Proper fraction   B) Improper fraction

C) Mixed fraction   D) Not a fraction

WORKSHEET 29

Equivalent fraction is a fraction with the same value as another fraction.

Examples:

$$\frac{1}{2} = \frac{2}{4} = \frac{4}{8}$$

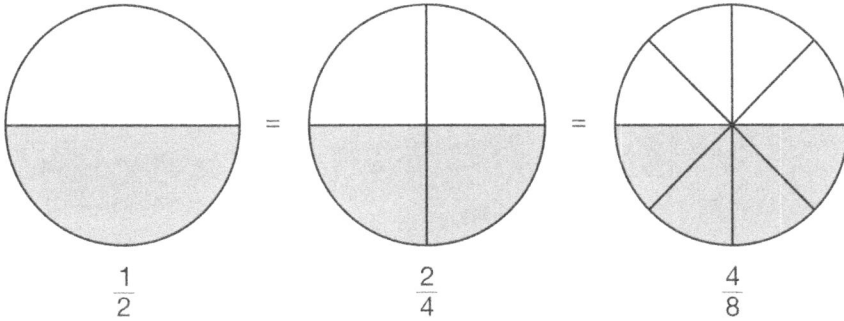

For questions 1 through 12, complete the equivalent fractions.

1. $\dfrac{1}{5} = \dfrac{\square}{10}$

2. $\dfrac{1}{6} = \dfrac{\square}{30}$

3. $\dfrac{1}{8} = \dfrac{\square}{80}$

4. $\dfrac{1}{7} = \dfrac{\square}{49}$

5. $\dfrac{1}{6} = \dfrac{\square}{150}$

6. $\dfrac{3}{5} = \dfrac{\square}{20}$

7. $\dfrac{5}{4} = \dfrac{\square}{40}$

8. $\dfrac{6}{7} = \dfrac{\square}{70}$

9. $\dfrac{8}{9} = \dfrac{\square}{90}$

10. $\dfrac{\square}{28} = \dfrac{1}{7}$

11. $\dfrac{18}{9} = \dfrac{6}{\square}$

12. $\dfrac{25}{150} = \dfrac{1}{\square}$

13. Which of following is equivalent to $\dfrac{1}{2}$?

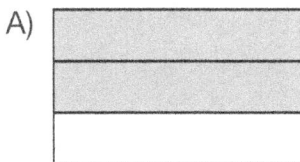

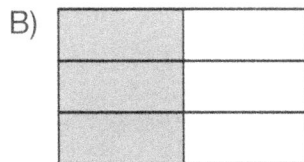

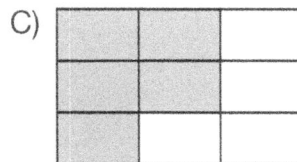

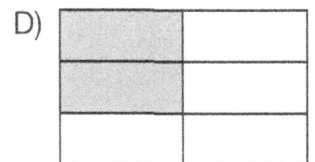

A)   B)   C)   D)

14. Which of the following fractions has the largest value?

A) $\dfrac{4}{5}$ B) $\dfrac{6}{7}$ C) $\dfrac{7}{8}$ D) $\dfrac{12}{11}$

15. Which of the following fractions is listed correctly?

A) $\dfrac{1}{2} = \dfrac{2}{3}$ B) $\dfrac{3}{2} = \dfrac{6}{18}$

C) $\dfrac{3}{2} = \dfrac{4}{9}$ D) $\dfrac{6}{5} = \dfrac{12}{10}$

Simplest Form

WORKSHEET 30

Simplify those fractions to their lowest terms.

1) $\dfrac{3}{6}$ = _____

2) $\dfrac{9}{18}$ = _____

3) $\dfrac{5}{15}$ = _____

4) $\dfrac{6}{18}$ = _____

5) $\dfrac{9}{27}$ = _____

6) $\dfrac{6}{30}$ = _____

7) $\dfrac{5}{20}$ = _____

8) $\dfrac{7}{21}$ = _____

9) $\dfrac{20}{30}$ = _____

10) $\dfrac{30}{40}$ = _____

11) $\dfrac{3}{21}$ = _____

12) $\dfrac{4}{20}$ = _____

13) $\dfrac{10}{40}$ = _____

14) $\dfrac{20}{50}$ = _____

AMERICAN MATH
ACADEMY

WORKSHEET 31

Cross-multiply and then compare the products.

Example: $\dfrac{1}{2}$ $<$ $\dfrac{3}{4}$ $\longrightarrow$ Cross multiply

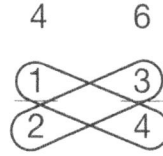

4   6

(1) ✕ (3)
(2) ✕ (4)

Because of 4 is less than 6, than $\dfrac{1}{2}$ is less than $\dfrac{3}{4}$

For questions 1 through 15 write >, = or < to compare the following fractions.

1) $\dfrac{1}{6}$ ◯ $\dfrac{3}{7}$

2) $\dfrac{4}{5}$ ◯ $\dfrac{3}{11}$

3) $\dfrac{5}{6}$ ◯ $\dfrac{8}{9}$

4) $\dfrac{12}{16}$ ◯ $\dfrac{13}{7}$

5) $\dfrac{9}{5}$ ◯ $\dfrac{13}{8}$

6) $\dfrac{7}{9}$ ◯ $\dfrac{6}{0}$

7) $\dfrac{21}{5}$ ◯ $\dfrac{8}{7}$

8) $\dfrac{7}{9}$ ◯ $\dfrac{4}{18}$

9) $\dfrac{42}{9}$ ◯ $\dfrac{19}{4}$

10) $\dfrac{40}{6}$ ◯ $\dfrac{50}{7}$

11) $\dfrac{70}{8}$ ◯ $\dfrac{16}{3}$

12) $\dfrac{90}{9}$ ◯ $\dfrac{40}{4}$

13) $\dfrac{10}{6}$ ◯ $\dfrac{10}{7}$

14) $\dfrac{20}{5}$ ◯ $\dfrac{16}{4}$

15) $\dfrac{30}{6}$ ◯ $\dfrac{20}{4}$

16) Which of following fractions has the largest value?

A) $\dfrac{1}{2}$ B) $\dfrac{2}{3}$

C) $\dfrac{4}{5}$ D) $\dfrac{5}{6}$

17) Which of the following fractions is listed correctly?

A) $\dfrac{1}{2} < \dfrac{2}{3}$ B) $\dfrac{3}{2} < \dfrac{6}{7}$

C) $\dfrac{5}{4} < \dfrac{8}{9}$ D) $\dfrac{6}{5} < \dfrac{10}{9}$

18) Which of following is $\dfrac{2}{3}$?

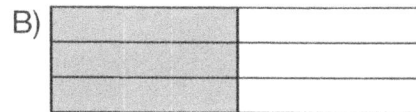

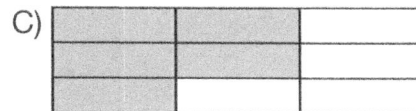

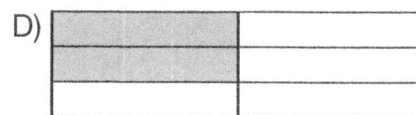

A)

B)

C)

D)

Ordering Fractions

Write the fractions in order from least to greatest.

1) $\dfrac{3}{4}$ $\quad$ $\dfrac{1}{4}$ $\quad$ $\dfrac{2}{4}$ $\quad$ = _____ _____ _____

2) $\dfrac{3}{9}$ $\quad$ $\dfrac{4}{9}$ $\quad$ $\dfrac{2}{9}$ $\quad$ = _____ _____ _____

3) $\dfrac{3}{8}$ $\quad$ $\dfrac{1}{4}$ $\quad$ $\dfrac{5}{8}$ $\quad$ = _____ _____ _____

4) $\dfrac{7}{10}$ $\quad$ $\dfrac{3}{5}$ $\quad$ $\dfrac{2}{3}$ $\quad$ = _____ _____ _____

5) $\dfrac{1}{3}$ $\quad$ $\dfrac{1}{4}$ $\quad$ $\dfrac{1}{5}$ $\quad$ = _____ _____ _____

6) $\dfrac{2}{3}$ $\quad$ $\dfrac{4}{5}$ $\quad$ $\dfrac{7}{10}$ $\quad$ = _____ _____ _____

7) $\dfrac{3}{4}$ $\quad$ $\dfrac{4}{5}$ $\quad$ $\dfrac{7}{10}$ $\quad$ = _____ _____ _____

8) $\dfrac{9}{2}$ $\quad$ $\dfrac{7}{2}$ $\quad$ $\dfrac{11}{2}$ $\quad$ = _____ _____ _____

9) $\dfrac{3}{5}$ $\quad$ $\dfrac{2}{7}$ $\quad$ $\dfrac{3}{2}$ $\quad$ = _____ _____ _____

AMERICAN MATH
—ACADEMY—

WORKSHEET 33

Adding Fractions: When you add fractions, if they have same denominator, you add numarators while keeping the denominator the same.

Example: $\dfrac{2}{3} + \dfrac{4}{3} = \dfrac{6}{3} = 2$ in simplest form.

For questions 1 through 21 add. Give the answer in simplest form.

1) $\dfrac{7}{3} + \dfrac{9}{3} =$ _____

2) $\dfrac{11}{20} + \dfrac{23}{20} =$ _____

3) $\dfrac{7}{19} + \dfrac{8}{19} =$ _____

4) $\dfrac{1}{4} + \dfrac{2}{4} =$ _____

5) $\dfrac{5}{6} + \dfrac{3}{6} =$ _____

6) $\dfrac{11}{7} + \dfrac{8}{7} =$ _____

7) $\dfrac{8}{11} + \dfrac{27}{11} =$ _____

8) $\dfrac{5}{20} + \dfrac{13}{20} =$ _____

9) $\dfrac{12}{17} + \dfrac{15}{17} =$ _____

10) $\dfrac{2}{15} + \dfrac{3}{15} =$ _____

11) $\dfrac{7}{30} + \dfrac{13}{30} =$ _____

12) $\dfrac{1}{19} + \dfrac{3}{19} =$ _____

13) $\dfrac{6}{14} + \dfrac{3}{14} =$ _____

14) $\dfrac{9}{40} + \dfrac{13}{40} =$ _____

15) $\dfrac{35}{17} + \dfrac{32}{17} =$ _____

16) $1\dfrac{1}{2} + 1\dfrac{1}{2} =$ _____

17) $2\dfrac{1}{2} + 3\dfrac{1}{2} =$ _____

18) $1\dfrac{1}{6} + \dfrac{5}{6} =$ _____

19) $1\dfrac{2}{3} + 1\dfrac{1}{3} =$ _____

20) $4\dfrac{1}{5} + 2\dfrac{1}{5} =$ _____

21) $5\dfrac{2}{7} + 1\dfrac{5}{7} =$ _____

Subtracting Fractions

Subtracting Fractions: When you subtract fractions that have the same denominators, you subtract only the numerators and keep the denominator the same.

Example: $\dfrac{5}{8} - \dfrac{3}{8} = \dfrac{5-3}{8} = \dfrac{2}{8} = \dfrac{1}{4}$ in simplest form.

For questions 1 through 21 subtract. Give the answer in simplest form.

1) $\dfrac{13}{3} - \dfrac{5}{3} =$ _____

2) $\dfrac{43}{30} - \dfrac{23}{30} =$ _____

3) $\dfrac{50}{19} - \dfrac{18}{19} =$ _____

4) $\dfrac{20}{4} - \dfrac{12}{4} =$ _____

5) $\dfrac{15}{6} - \dfrac{9}{6} =$ _____

6) $\dfrac{33}{7} - \dfrac{27}{7} =$ _____

7) $\dfrac{51}{11} - \dfrac{47}{11} =$ _____

8) $\dfrac{60}{20} - \dfrac{18}{20} =$ _____

9) $\dfrac{75}{17} - \dfrac{45}{17} =$ _____

10) $\dfrac{42}{15} - \dfrac{38}{15} =$ _____

11) $\dfrac{77}{30} - \dfrac{53}{30} =$ _____

12) $\dfrac{79}{19} - \dfrac{17}{19} =$ _____

13) $\dfrac{48}{14} - \dfrac{47}{14} =$ _____

14) $\dfrac{100}{40} - \dfrac{89}{40} =$ _____

15) $\dfrac{19}{7} - \dfrac{12}{7} =$ _____

16) $2\dfrac{1}{2} - \dfrac{1}{2} =$ _____

17) $1\dfrac{5}{10} - \dfrac{4}{10} =$ _____

18) $1\dfrac{1}{6} - \dfrac{5}{6} =$ _____

19) $2\dfrac{1}{3} - 1\dfrac{1}{3} =$ _____

20) $3\dfrac{1}{4} - 1\dfrac{1}{4} =$ _____

21) $5\dfrac{1}{5} - 2\dfrac{1}{5} =$ _____

AMERICAN MATH
— ACADEMY —

WORKSHEET 35

Add.

1) $1\dfrac{1}{4} + 1\dfrac{1}{4} =$ _____

2) $3\dfrac{1}{5} + 2\dfrac{1}{5} =$ _____

3) $4\dfrac{1}{6} + 3\dfrac{1}{6} =$ _____

4) $7\dfrac{1}{5} + 3\dfrac{1}{5} =$ _____

5) $1\dfrac{1}{8} + 1\dfrac{3}{8} =$ _____

6) $4\dfrac{1}{5} + 3\dfrac{3}{5} =$ _____

7) $1\dfrac{2}{7} + 3\dfrac{4}{7} =$ _____

8) $1\dfrac{3}{8} + 3\dfrac{5}{8} =$ _____

9) $10\dfrac{1}{10} + 2\dfrac{7}{10} =$ _____

10) $8\dfrac{1}{4} + 5\dfrac{1}{4} =$ _____

11) $9\dfrac{1}{3} + 3\dfrac{1}{3} =$ _____

12) $7\dfrac{1}{7} + 3\dfrac{1}{7} =$ _____

13) $11\dfrac{1}{4} + 12\dfrac{1}{4} =$ _____

14) $12\dfrac{1}{2} + 11\dfrac{1}{2} =$ _____

15) $16\dfrac{1}{2} + 18\dfrac{1}{2} =$ _____

16) $6\dfrac{1}{8} + 7\dfrac{1}{8} =$ _____

Subtracting Mixed Numbers

WORKSHEET 36

Subtract. Regroup, if necessary.

1) $1\dfrac{2}{3} - 1\dfrac{1}{3} =$ _____

2) $6\dfrac{1}{3} - 2\dfrac{1}{3} =$ _____

3) $7\dfrac{1}{4} - 2\dfrac{3}{4} =$ _____

4) $8\dfrac{4}{5} - 4\dfrac{2}{5} =$ _____

5) $6\dfrac{1}{3} - 4\dfrac{1}{3} =$ _____

6) $9\dfrac{1}{10} - 8\dfrac{1}{10} =$ _____

7) $8\dfrac{1}{9} - 4\dfrac{2}{9} =$ _____

8) $5\dfrac{1}{6} - 2\dfrac{1}{6} =$ _____

9) $8\dfrac{1}{4} - 4\dfrac{1}{4} =$ _____

10) $10\dfrac{1}{8} - 7\dfrac{1}{8} =$ _____

11) $12\dfrac{1}{5} - 7\dfrac{1}{5} =$ _____

12) $7\dfrac{1}{4} - 3\dfrac{1}{4} =$ _____

13) $9\dfrac{1}{7} - 6\dfrac{1}{7} =$ _____

14) $\dfrac{12}{3} - 2\dfrac{1}{3} =$ _____

15) $9 - 2\dfrac{1}{5} =$ _____

16) $2\dfrac{1}{3} - \dfrac{2}{3} =$ _____

AMERICAN MATH
ACADEMY

WORKSHEET 37

Step by step: • Multiply the numerators,
• Multiply the denominators,
• Simplify the fraction if needed.

Example: $2\frac{1}{4} \times 2\frac{1}{3} = \frac{9}{4} \times \frac{7}{3} = \frac{9 \times 7}{4 \times 3} = \frac{63 \div 3}{12 \div 3} = \frac{21}{4} = 5\frac{1}{4}$

For questions 1 through 21 multiply. Give the answer in simplest form.

1) $\frac{1}{3} \times \frac{5}{2} =$ _____

2) $\frac{5}{10} \times \frac{7}{30} =$ _____

3) $\frac{10}{9} \times \frac{1}{8} =$ _____

4) $\frac{7}{3} \times \frac{1}{7} =$ _____

5) $\frac{5}{9} \times \frac{6}{9} =$ _____

6) $\frac{3}{4} \times \frac{1}{18} =$ _____

7) $\frac{1}{11} \times \frac{33}{4} =$ _____

8) $\frac{1}{10} \times \frac{30}{8} =$ _____

9) $\frac{5}{17} \times \frac{51}{3} =$ _____

10) $\frac{2}{5} \times \frac{3}{4} =$ _____

11) $\frac{8}{3} \times \frac{3}{2} =$ _____

12) $\frac{11}{100} \times \frac{10}{40} =$ _____

13) $1\frac{1}{2} \times \frac{7}{3} =$ _____

14) $\frac{1}{12} \times \frac{3}{7} =$ _____

15) $1\frac{1}{7} \times \frac{14}{8} =$ _____

16) $2\frac{1}{2} \times \frac{1}{4} =$ _____

17) $1\frac{1}{4} \times 1\frac{1}{3} =$ _____

18) $1\frac{1}{6} \times \frac{3}{5} =$ _____

19) $2\frac{1}{3} \times 1\frac{1}{7} =$ _____

20) $3\frac{1}{4} \times 1\frac{1}{13} =$ _____

21) $5\frac{1}{8} \times 2\frac{1}{41} =$ _____

Mixed Fraction Operations

WORKSHEET 38

Add, subract or multiply. Regroup, if necessary.

1) $4\frac{3}{5} + 1\frac{2}{5} = $ _____

2) $\frac{6}{5} - \frac{3}{5} = $ _____

3) $\frac{3}{4} \times \frac{4}{6} = $ _____

4) $1\frac{1}{5} + 1\frac{2}{5} = $ _____

5) $\frac{1}{4} \times 1\frac{1}{4} = $ _____

6) $\frac{11}{3} \times \frac{5}{3} = $ _____

7) $6\frac{1}{2} - \frac{1}{2} = $ _____

8) $\frac{8}{7} \times \frac{3}{4} = $ _____

9) $1\frac{1}{3} + 1\frac{2}{3} = $ _____

10) $4\frac{1}{4} - 3\frac{1}{4} = $ _____

11) $5\frac{2}{3} + 3\frac{1}{3} = $ _____

12) $4\frac{1}{4} - 3\frac{1}{4} = $ _____

13) $\frac{3}{5} \times \frac{4}{7} = $ _____

14) $4\frac{1}{3} + 4\frac{1}{3} = $ _____

15) $8\frac{1}{5} - 4\frac{3}{5} = $ _____

16) $9 \times \frac{3}{8} = $ _____

AMERICAN MATH
ACADEMY

WORKSHEET 39

1. A grocery store bought 45 pounds of tomatoes and sold $\frac{5}{9}$ on the same day. At the end of the day, how many pounds of tomatoes where left?

   A) 25 pounds

   B) 20 pounds

   C) 45 pounds

   D) 81 pounds

2. There are 24 students in math class. If $\frac{2}{3}$ of the students in this class are male students, find the number of female students in the math class?

   A) 6

   B) 8

   C) 12

   D) 16

3. The width of a rectangular garden is $1\frac{2}{3}$ cm. The length is $1\frac{4}{5}$ cm. Which of the following is the area of the garden?

   A) $\frac{1}{3}$ cm²

   B) 3 cm²

   C) $\frac{2}{3}$ cm²

   D) 4 cm²

4. Tony has 12 pencils and wants to give $\frac{3}{4}$ of them to a friend while keeping the rest for himself. How many pencils would his friend get?

   A) 3

   B) 6

   C) 8

   D) 9

5. Last night, Tony spent $1\frac{1}{8}$ hours doing his math homework. John did his math homework for $\frac{1}{4}$ as many hours as Tony did. How many hours did John spend on his homework?

   A) $\frac{9}{32}$

   B) $4\frac{1}{2}$

   C) $\frac{3}{8}$

   D) $\frac{3}{16}$

Understanding Decimals

Examples:

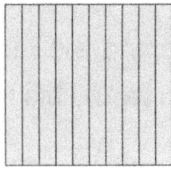

1

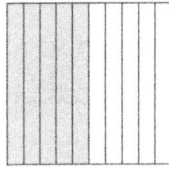

$\frac{5}{10}$

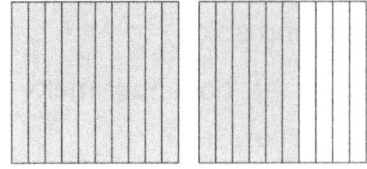

1.7

Fill in the grid to show the decimal.

1)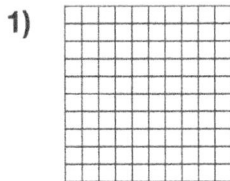

1

2)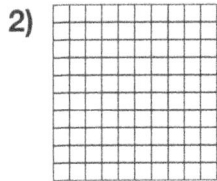

0.54

3)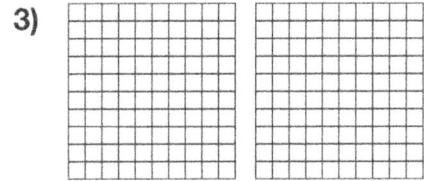

1.9

4)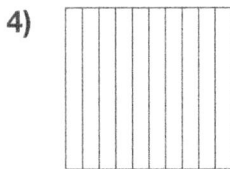

0.7

5)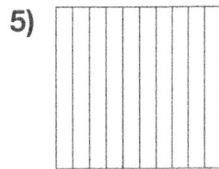

0.4

6)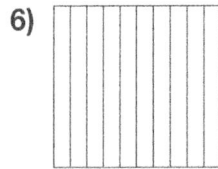

1

7)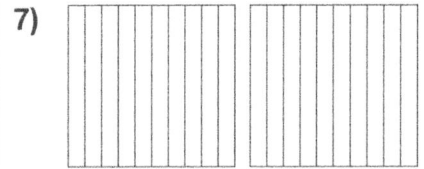

1.8

8)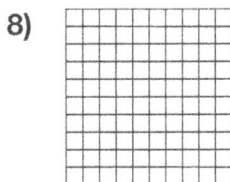

0.43

9)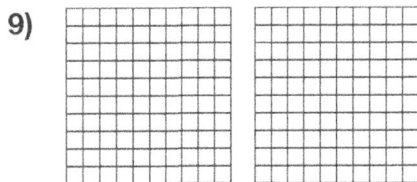

1 and 19 hundredths

10)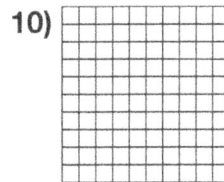

35 hundredths

11)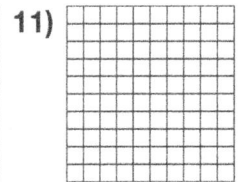

0,73

Write the decimal represented by the grid.

12)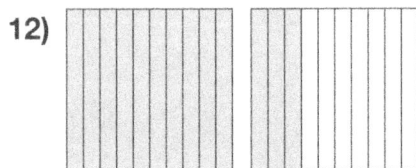

13)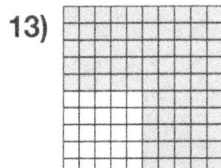

14)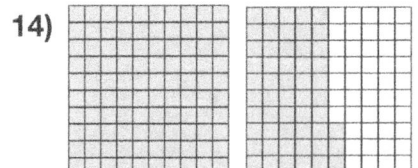

AMERICAN MATH
—ACADEMY—

WORKSHEET 41

Examples:

$\dfrac{8}{10}$ = **0.8** $\dfrac{7}{100}$ = **0.07**   0.4 = $\dfrac{4}{10}$ = $\dfrac{2}{5}$ 0.63 = $\dfrac{63}{100}$

Write these fractions as decimals.

1) $\dfrac{4}{10}$ = ☐

2) $\dfrac{8}{10}$ = ☐

3) $1\dfrac{1}{10}$ = ☐

4) $\dfrac{5}{10}$ = ☐

5) $\dfrac{7}{10}$ = ☐

6) $3\dfrac{2}{10}$ = ☐

7) $\dfrac{3}{5}$ = ☐

8) $\dfrac{10}{10}$ = ☐

9) $4\dfrac{1}{10}$ = ☐

Write these decimals as fractions.

10) 0.3 = $\dfrac{3}{\boxed{}}$

11) 0.4 = $\dfrac{4}{\boxed{}}$

12) 0.7 = $\dfrac{7}{\boxed{}}$

13) 0.5 = $\dfrac{5}{\boxed{}}$ = $\dfrac{1}{\boxed{}}$

14) 0.8 = $\dfrac{8}{\boxed{}}$ = $\dfrac{4}{\boxed{}}$

15) 0.2 = $\dfrac{2}{\boxed{}}$ = $\dfrac{1}{\boxed{}}$

16) 0.9 = $\dfrac{9}{\boxed{}}$

17) 0.6 = $\dfrac{6}{\boxed{}}$ = $\dfrac{3}{\boxed{}}$

18) $1\dfrac{1}{10}$ = $\dfrac{11}{\boxed{}}$

Change these fractions to decimals and decimals to fractions.

19) $\dfrac{73}{100}$ = ☐

20) $\dfrac{12}{100}$ = ☐

21) $\dfrac{88}{100}$ = ☐

22) $\dfrac{90}{100}$ = ☐

23) $\dfrac{35}{100}$ = ☐

24) $\dfrac{77}{100}$ = ☐

25) 0.47 = ☐

26) 0.71 = ☐

27) 1.9 = ☐

28) 0.61 = ☐

29) 0.46 = ☐

30) 1.18 = ☐

Comparing Decimals

Example: Which number is greater 43.43 or 43.23 ?

$\begin{array}{c} 43.43 \\ 43.23 \end{array} >$ Line up the numbers then compare the digits that are different.

$\begin{array}{c} 43.43 \\ 43.23 \end{array}$ Since 4 is greater than 2. So 43.43 is greater than 43.23

$= 43.43 > 43.23$

Compare each pair of decimals using the symbols >, < or =.

1) 40.5 ☐ 40.10

2) 50.3 ☐ 50.30

3) 22.3 ☐ 22.03

4) 3.5 ☐ 3.55

5) 5.16 ☐ 5.20

6) 12.30 ☐ 12.35

7) 47.33 ☐ 45.6

8) 24.8 ☐ 24.08

9) 54.7 ☐ 53.8

10) 1.01 ☐ 1.001

11) 36.40 ☐ 36.04

12) 54.5 ☐ 55.4

13) 11.7 ☐ 11.8

14) 9.6 ☐ 9.60

AMERICAN MATH
—ACADEMY—

WORKSHEET 43

Length and Distance	Weight	Capacity
10 millimeter = 1 centimeter 100 centimeter = 1 meter 1000 meter = 1 kilometer	1000 gram = 1 kilogram 1000 kilogram = 1 metric ton	1000 milliliter = 1 liter 1000 liter = 1 kiloliter

Complete each table.

1)

Liters	Milliliters
10	
20	
30	
40	
50	

2)

Kilograms	Grams
5	
10	
15	
20	
25	

3)

Meters	Centimeters
5	
10	
15	
20	
25	

4)

Centimeters	Millimeters
2	
4	
6	
8	
10	

5)

Tons	Kilograms
1	
2	
3	
4	
5	

6)

Kiloliters	Liters
1	
2	
3	
4	
5	

Converting Customary Units

WORKSHEET 44

Length	Weight
1 feet = 12 inches 1 yard = 3 feet 1 mile = 5.280 feet 1 mile = 1,760 yards	1 pound = 16 ounces 1 ton = 2,000 pounds 1 gallon = 4 quarters 1 quart = 2 pints

Complete each table.

1)

Gallons	Quarters
1	
2	
3	
4	
5	

2)

Feet	Inches
1	
2	
3	
4	
5	

3)

Gallons	Pints
2	
4	
6	
8	
10	

4)

Yards	Feet
3	
6	
9	
12	
15	

5)

Pounds	Ounces
5	
10	
15	
20	
25	

6)

Tons	Pounds
5	
10	
15	
20	
25	

AMERICAN MATH
—ACADEMY—

WORKSHEET 45

Time Conversion Table

1 minute	= 60 seconds	1 week	= 7 days
1 hour	= 60 minutes	1 year	= 12 months
1 day	= 24 hours	1 year	= 52 weeks

Convert into given units of measurement.

1) 15 hours = _____ minutes

2) 20 hours = _____ minutes

3) 18 minutes = _____ seconds

4) 10 days = _____ hours

5) 300 seconds = _____ minutes

6) 360 hours = _____ days

7) 30 days = _____ hours

8) 12 weeks = _____ days

9) 1200 hours = _____ days

10) 4 days = _____ minutes

11) 60 seconds = _____ minute

12) 11 days = _____ hours

13) 5 weeks = _____ days

14) 4 years = _____ weeks

15) 600 seconds = _____ minutes

16) 2 weeks = _____ hours

17) 6 weeks = _____ days

18) 6 years = _____ months

19) 120 minutes = _____ seconds

20) 3 years = _____ days

ANGELS

Acute Angle: An angle that is less than 90° but greater than 0°

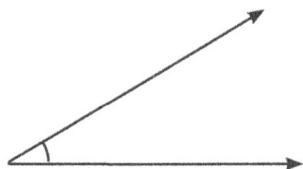

Right Angle: An angle that is exactly 90°

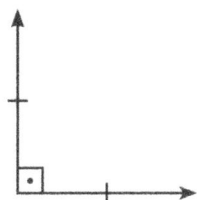

Obtuse Angle: An angle that is greater than 90° but less than 180°

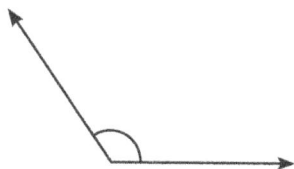

Straight Angle: An angle that is exactly 180°

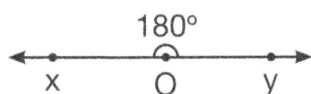

AMERICAN MATH
— ACADEMY —

WORKSHEET 46

Label each of following angles as acute, obtuse, right or straight.

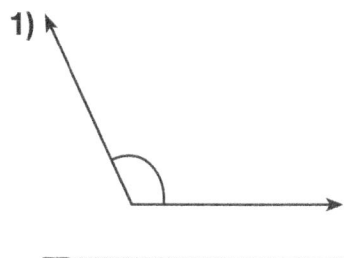

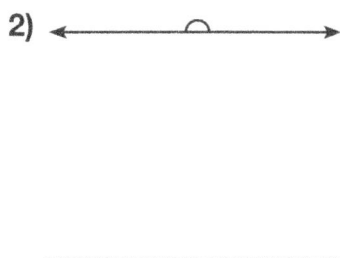

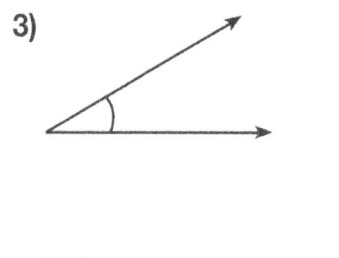

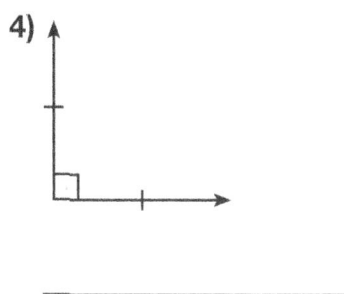

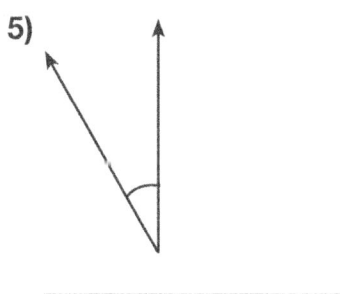

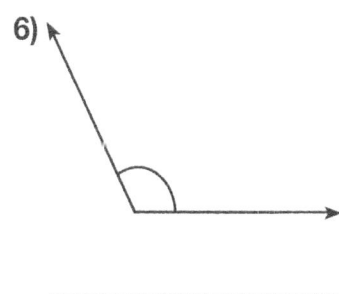

1)

_____

2)

_____

3)

_____

4)

_____

5)

_____

6)

_____

Write line, line segment or ray for each of following lines.

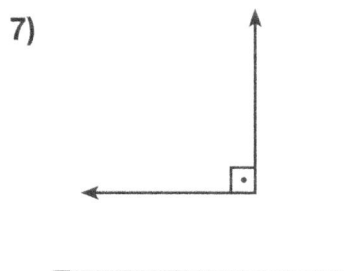

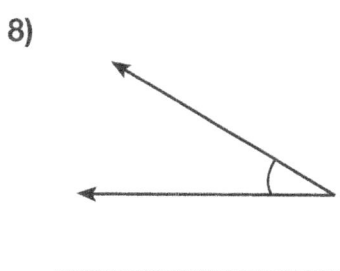

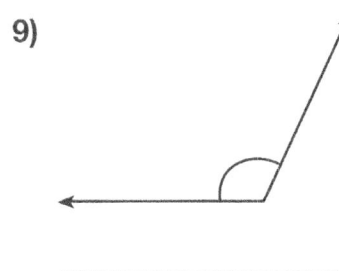

7)

_____

8)

_____

9)

_____

Write Parallel, perpendicular or intersect for each of following lines.

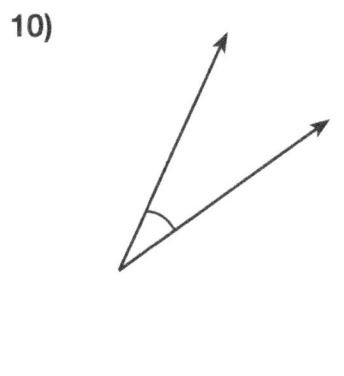

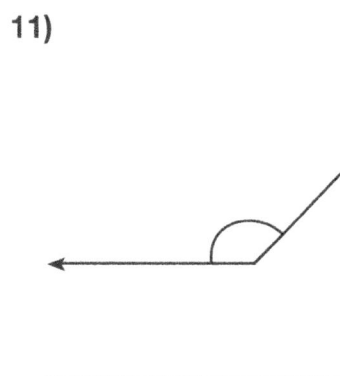

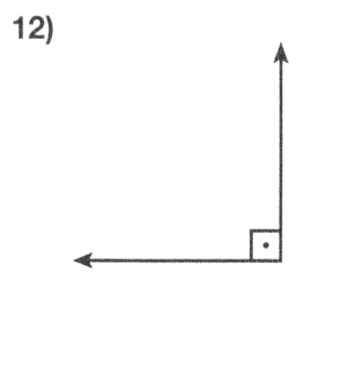

10)

_____

11)

_____

12)

_____

Angels

Write the measure of each combined angle.

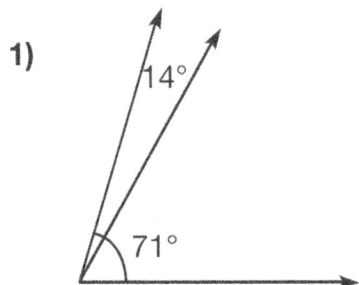

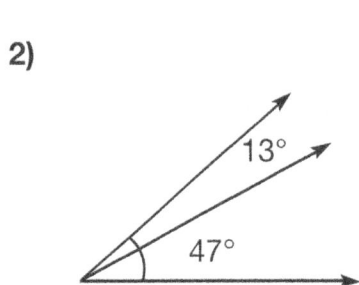

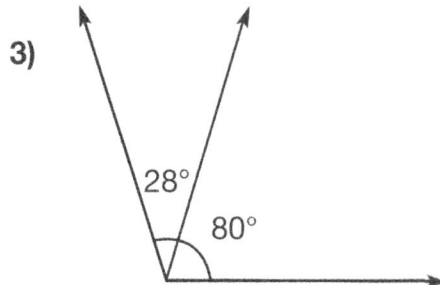

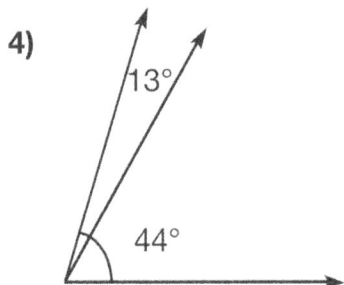

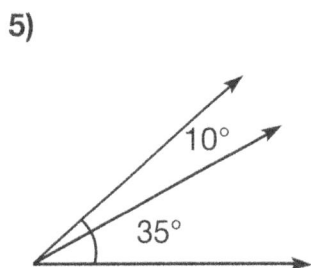

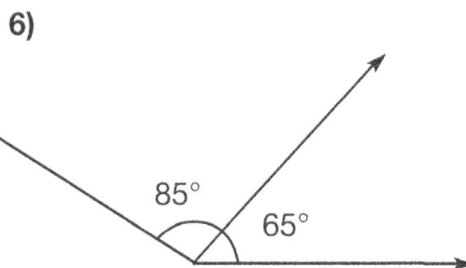

1)

14°

71°

2)

13°

47°

3)

28°

80°

4)

13°

44°

5)

10°

35°

6)

85°

65°

7) Combined angle measure = 140°

85°

8) Combined angle measure = 105°

44°

9) Combined angle measure = 76°

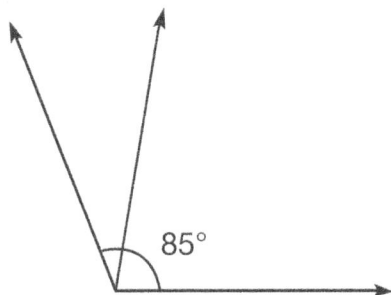

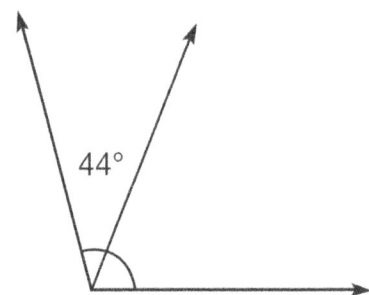

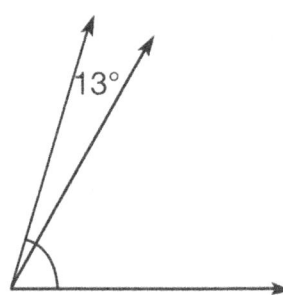

13°

Classifying Triangles

Acute triangle

All angle are less then 90°

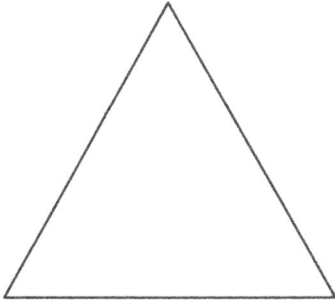

Right triangle

One angle is 90°

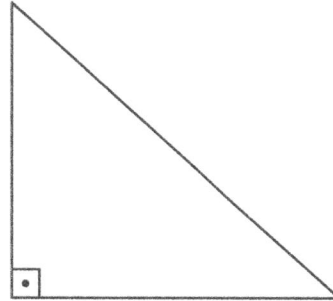

Obtuse triangle

One angle is greater 90° but less than 180°

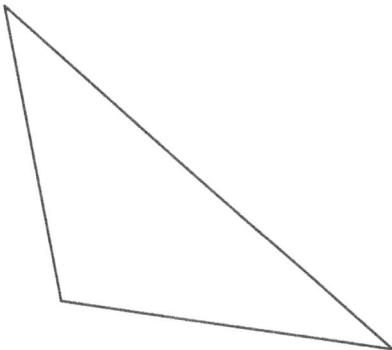

Equilateral triangle

All the three sides are equal.

All the three angles are equal to 60°

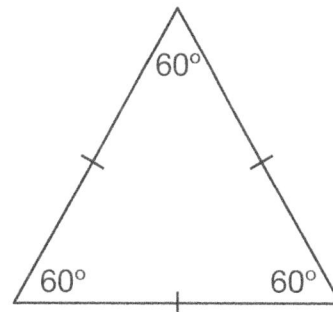

60°

60° 60°

Isosceles triangle

At least any two sides are equal.

Any two angles are equal.

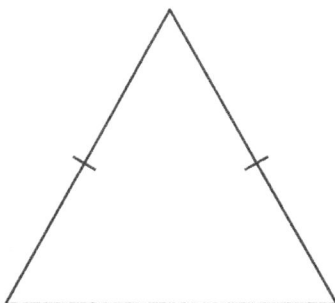

Scalene triangle

All three sides have different lengths.

All three angles are unequal.

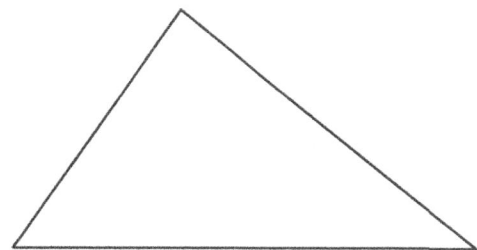

Classifying Triangles

WORKSHEET 48

Classify each of following triangle as acute, obtuse, equilateral, scalene, or isosceles triangle base on sides.

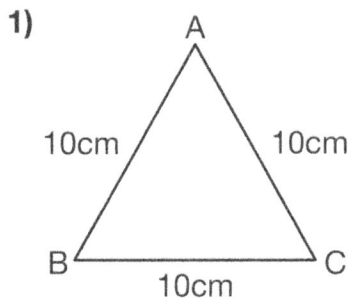

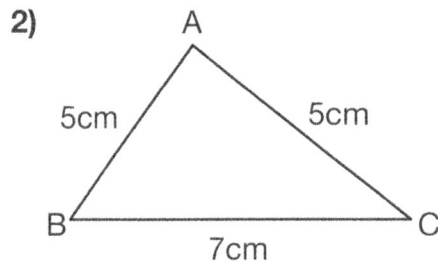

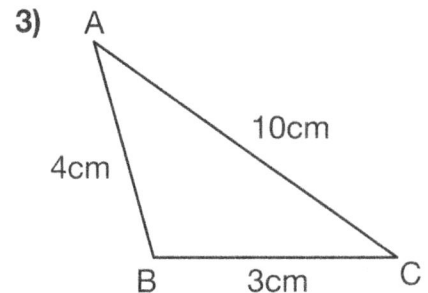

1)

A, B, C triangle with sides 10cm, 10cm, 10cm

_____

2)

A, B, C triangle with sides 5cm, 5cm, 7cm

_____

3)

A, B, C triangle with sides 4cm, 10cm, 3cm

_____

Classify each of following triangle as acute, obtuse, equilateral, scalene, or isosceles triangle base on angles.

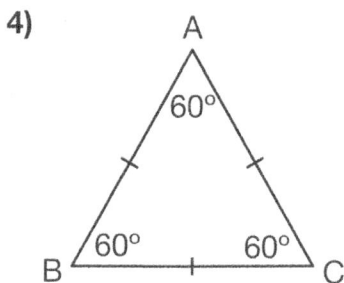

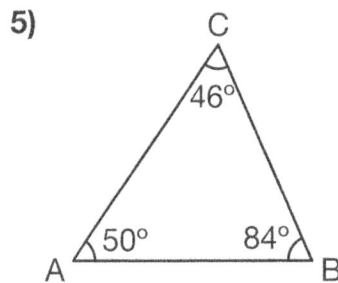

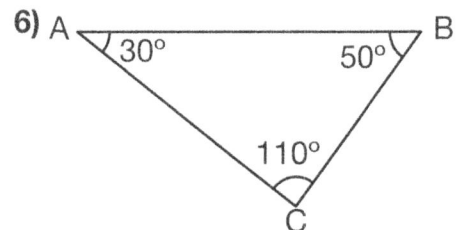

4)

Triangle with angles 60°, 60°, 60°

_____

5)

Triangle with angles 46°, 50°, 84°

_____

6)

Triangle with angles 30°, 50°, 110°

_____

Classify each of following triangle base on angles, and sides.

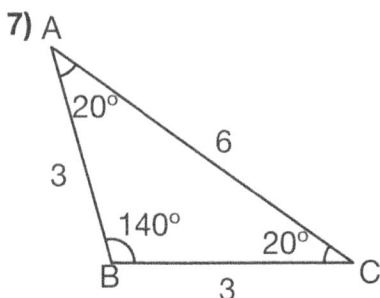

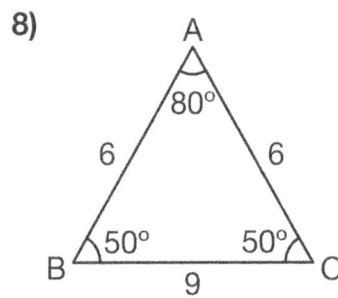

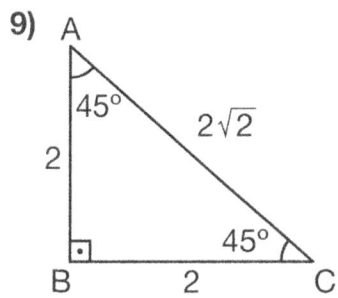

7)

Triangle with angles 20°, 140°, 20° and sides 3, 6, 3

_____

8)

Triangle with angles 80°, 50°, 50° and sides 6, 6, 9

_____

9)

Triangle with angles 45°, 90°, 45° and sides 2, $2\sqrt{2}$, 2

_____

AMERICAN MATH
—ACADEMY—

Classifying Quadrilaterals

Quadrilaterals: A quadrilateral is a polygon with four sides and 4 angles.

Parallelogram

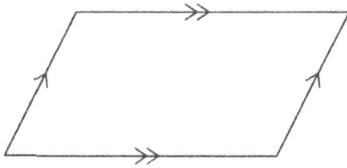

4 sides

4 angles

Opposite sides are parallel

Opposite sides are equal

Rectangle

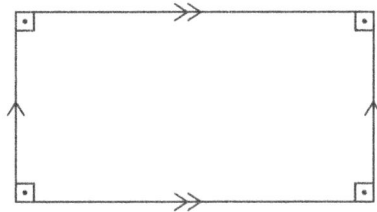

4 sides

4 right angles

Opposite sides are parallel

Opposite sides are equal

Trapezoid

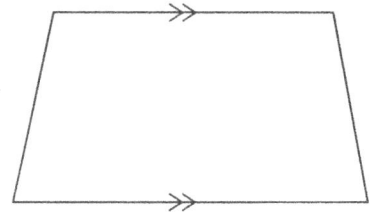

4 sides

4 different angles

Only one pair of sides is parallel

All sides are not equal

Rhombus

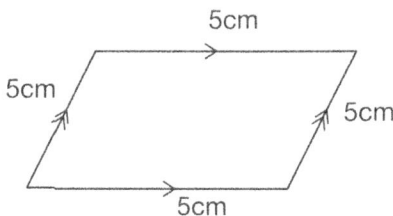

4 sides

4 angles

Opposite sides are parallel

All sides are equal

Square

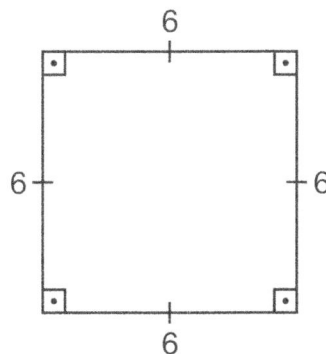

4 sides

4 right angles

Opposite sides are parallel

All sides are equal

Kite

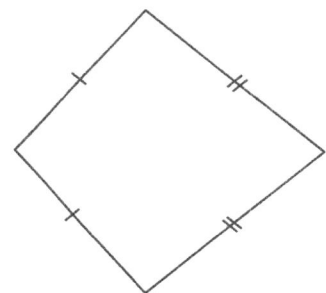

4 sides

4 angles

No parallel sides

2 sides are equal

Classifying Quadrilaterals Practice

Classify each of quadrilaterals from following table.

Grouping	Sides	Angles	Parallel Sides
Rectangle			
Square			
Trapezoid			
Rhombus			
Parallelogram			
Kite			

WORKSHEET 50

Draw the line of **symmetry** for each shape. (Note: some shape can be cut more than one way).

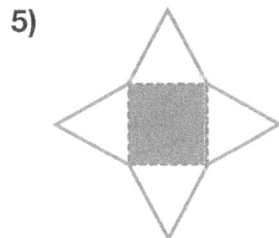

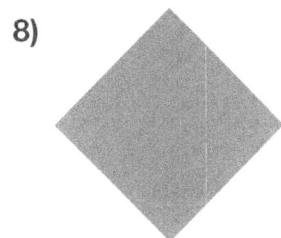

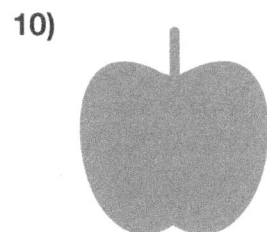

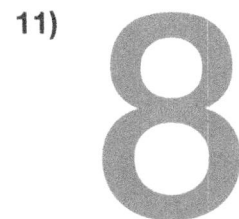

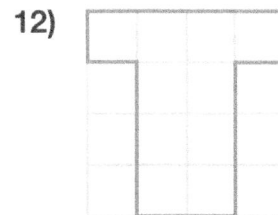

1) K

2) M

3) X

4) ♥

5) ◆

6) Z

7) ■

8) ◆

9) ▲

10) 🍎

11) 8

12) T

Perimeter of Shapes

WORKSHEET 51

Find the perimeter of each shape.

1)

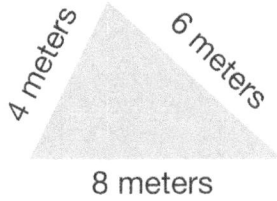

4 meters   6 meters

8 meters

_____ meters

2)

11 inches

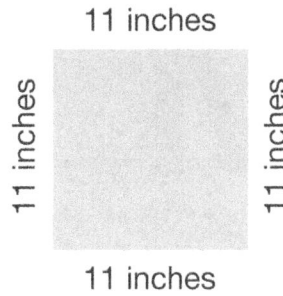

11 inches   11 inches

11 inches

_____ inches

3)

4 yards

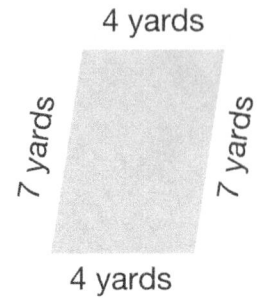

7 yards   7 yards

4 yards

_____ yards

4)

3 feet

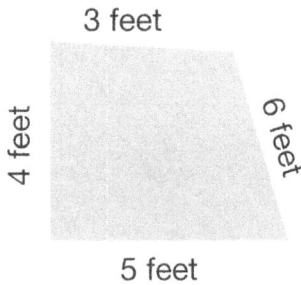

4 feet   6 feet

5 feet

_____ feet

5)

6 meters

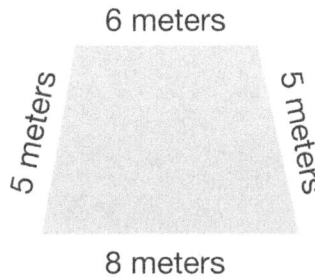

5 meters   5 meters

8 meters

_____ meters

6)

4 feet

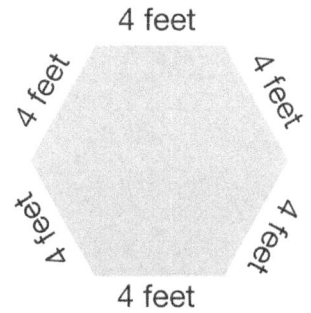

4 feet   4 feet

4 feet   4 feet

4 feet

_____ feet

7)

9 inches

7 inches   7 inches

9 inches

_____ inches

8)

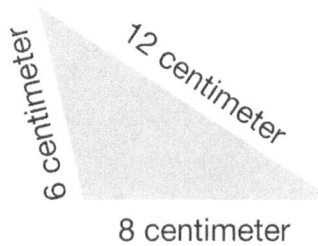

6 centimeter   12 centimeter

8 centimeter

_____ centimeter

9)

6 inches   6 inches

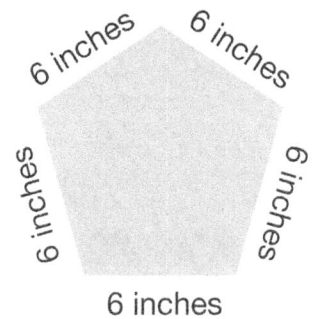

6 inches   6 inches

6 inches

_____ inches

AMERICAN MATH
ACADEMY

WORKSHEET 52

For questions 1 through 12 find **perimeter** of each shape.

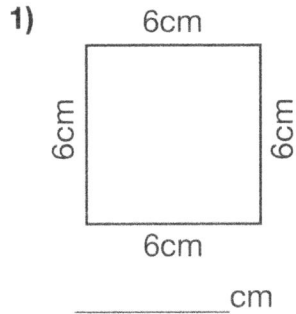

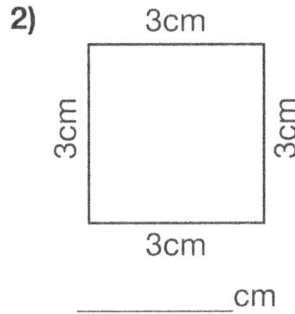

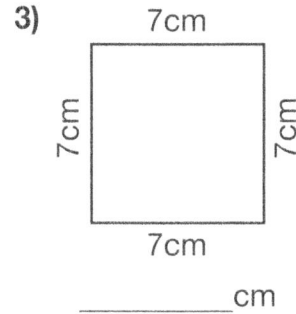

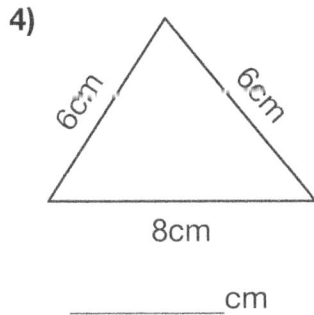

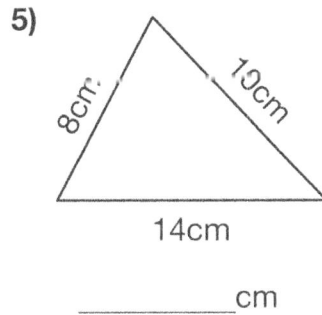

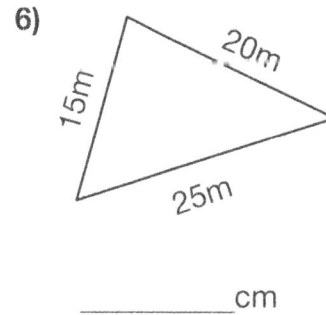

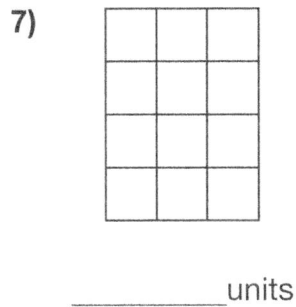

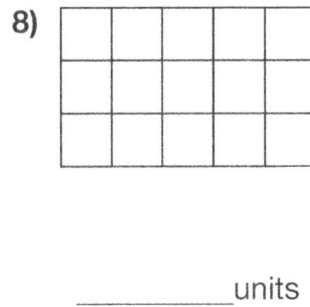

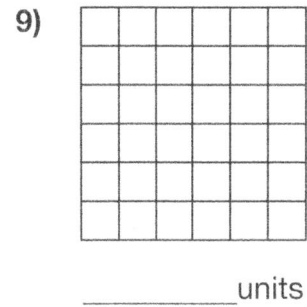

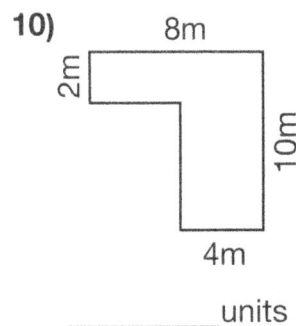

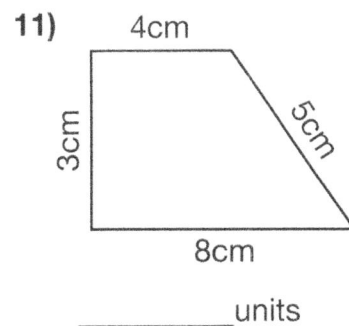

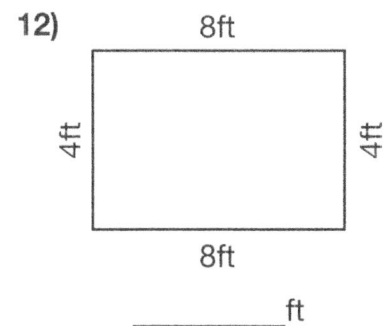

1)

6cm
6cm
6cm
6cm

_____cm

2)

3cm
3cm
3cm
3cm

_____cm

3)

7cm
7cm
7cm
7cm

_____cm

4)

6cm
6cm
8cm

_____cm

5)

8cm
10cm
14cm

_____cm

6)

15m
20m
25m

_____cm

7)

_____units

8)

_____units

9)

_____units

10)

8m
2m
10m
4m

_____units

11)

4cm
3cm
5cm
8cm

_____units

12)

8ft
4ft
4ft
8ft

_____ft

Area of Shapes

WORKSHEET 53

For questions 1 through 12 find **area** of each shape.

1)
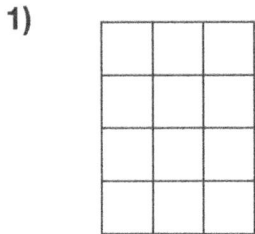

_____square units

2)
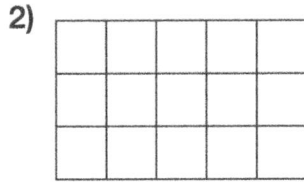

_____square units

3)
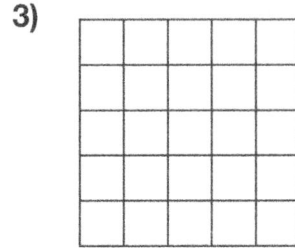

_____square units

4)
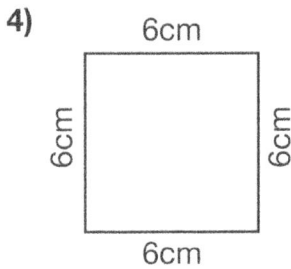

_____cm^2

5)
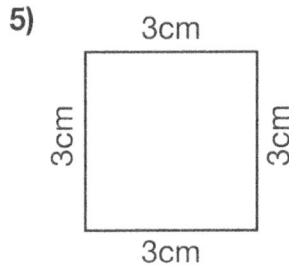

_____cm^2

6)
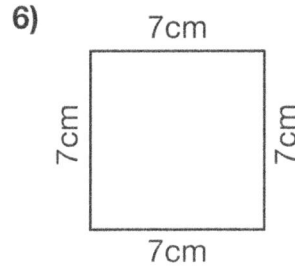

_____cm^2

7)
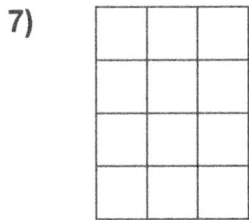

_____square units

8)
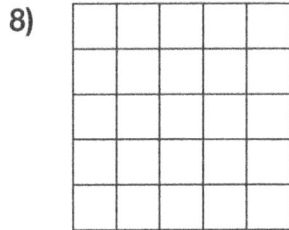

_____square units

9)
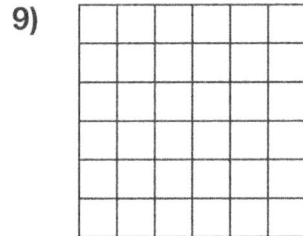

_____square units

10)
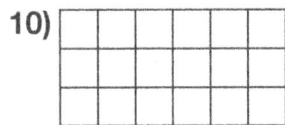

_____square units

11)
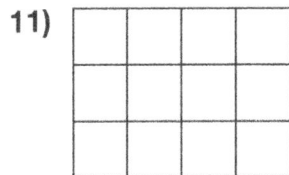

_____square units

12)
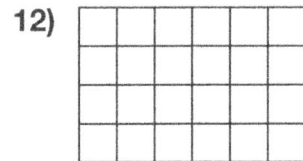

_____square units

AMERICAN MATH
—ACADEMY—

WORKSHEET 54

1)

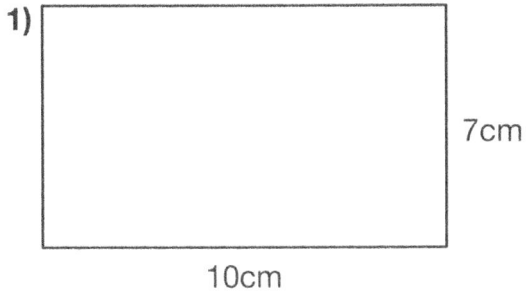

Area: _____ cm²

Perimeter: _____ cm

2)

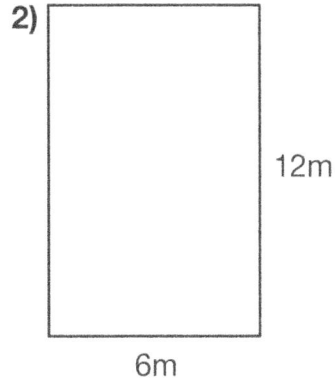

Area: _____ m²

Perimeter: _____ m

3)

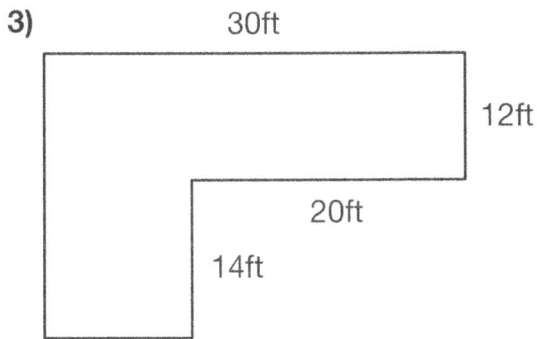

Area: _____ ft²

Perimeter: _____ ft

4)

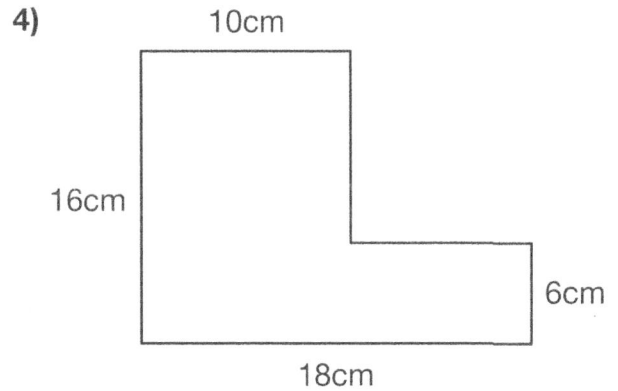

Area: _____ cm²

Perimeter: _____ cm

5)

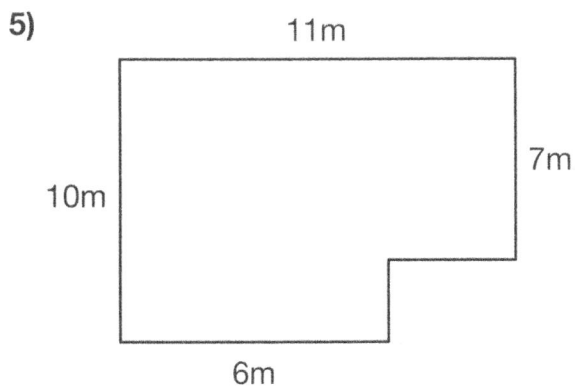

Area: _____ m²

Perimeter: _____ m

Coordinate System

Coordinate System: A coordinate system formed by the intersection of a vertical number line, called the y-axis, and a horizontal number line, called the x-axis.

Origin: A beginning or starting point. The point where lines intersect each other at (0, 0).

Ordered pair: A pair of numbers that can be used to locate a point on a coordinate plane.
The order of the numbers in a pair is important, and the x-axis always comes before the y-axis.

Example: (3, 5)

x-coordinate: The first number in an ordered pair is called the x-coordinate.

Example: (4,0)

y-coordinate: The second number in an ordered pair is called the y-coordinate.

Example: (0,7)

WORKSHEET 55

1) List the coordinates for each given point.

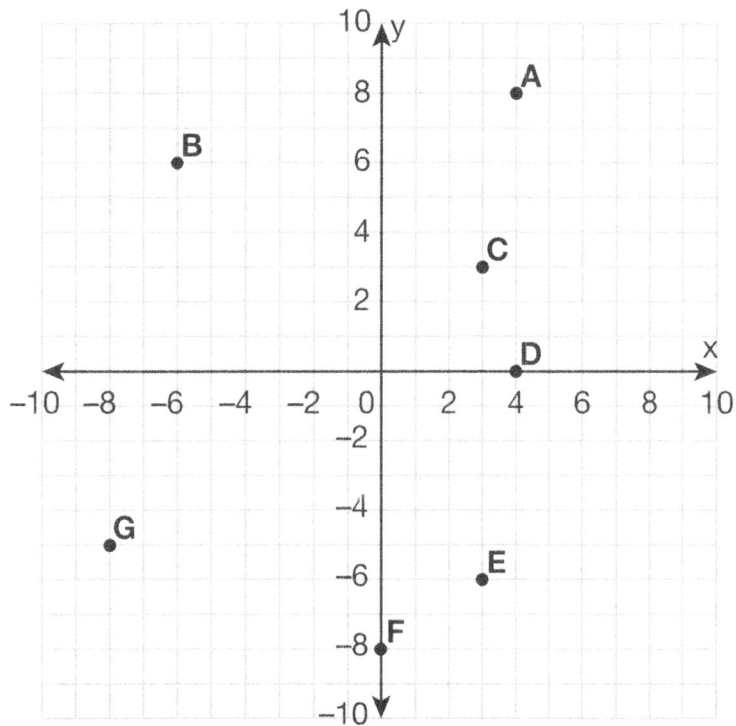

Coordinates	Point
	A
	B
	C
	D
	E
	F
	G

2) Which ordered pair locates a point on the y-axis?

A) (1, 1)   B) (1, 0)   C) (3, 0)   D) (0, − 1)

3) Which ordered pair locates a point on the x-axis?

A) (3, 1)   B) (4, 0)   C) (3, 6)   D) (0, 8)

4) Which ordered pair located at origin?

A) (5, 2)   B) (7, 0)   C) (3, 0)   D) (0, 0)

1. What is the value of the digit 5 in the number 5,843?

A) 5

B) 50

C) 500

D) 5,000

2. In the number 6,125, which digit is in the thousands place?

A) 6

B) 1

C) 2

D) 5

3. What is the digit in the tens place in the number 7,368?

A) 7

B) 3

C) 6

D) 8

4. Which of the following numbers is the smallest?

A) 4,256

B) 4,562

C) 4,625

D) 4,265

5. Compare: 9,427 ____ 9,742

A) < (less than)

B) > (greater than)

C) = (equal to)

6. If a number has the digit 3 in the hundreds place, is it greater or less than a number with 5 in the hundreds place?

A) Greater

B) Less

C) Equal

American Math Academy

7. Arrange the following numbers in ascending order: 3,712; 3,127; 3,721

A) 3,127; 3,712; 3,721

B) 3,721; 3,127; 3,712

C) 3,127; 3,721; 3,712

8. Put the following numbers in descending order: 8,945; 8,549; 8,954

A) 8,954; 8,945; 8,549

B) 8,549; 8,945; 8,954

C) 8,549; 8,945

9. What number comes between 6,978 and 6,980?

A) 6,979

B) 6,981

C) 6,977

10. Round 4,643 to the nearest hundred.

A) 4,600

B) 4,640

C) 4,700

11. If you round 5,286 to the nearest thousand, what do you get?

A) 5,200

B) 5,300

C) 5,000

12. Round 2,379 to the nearest ten.

A) 2,370

B) 2,380

C) 2,400

American Math Academy

13. If you round 8,765 to the nearest ten, what do you get?

A) 8,760

B) 8,770

C) 8,800

16. What is the value of the digit 7 in the number 7,812?

A) 7

B) 70

C) 700

D) 7,000

14. In the number 8,734, which digit is in the thousands place?

A) 8

B) 7

C) 3

D) 4

Comparing Numbers:

17. Compare: 6,375 ___ 6,573

A) < (less than)

B) > (greater than)

C) = (equal to)

15. What is the digit in the thousands place in the number 9,562?

A) 9

B) 5

C) 6

D) 2

18. If a number has the digit 9 in the tens place, is it greater or less than a number with 9 in the hundreds place?

A) Greater

B) Less

C) Equal

American Math Academy

19. Arrange the following numbers in ascending order: 4,925; 4,259; 4,592

A) 4,259; 4,592; 4,925

B) 4,925; 4,259; 4,592

C) 4,259; 4,925; 4,592

22. If you round 3,489 to the nearest thousand, what do you get?

A) 3,000

B) 3,500

C) 4,000

20. Put the following numbers in descending order: 6,732; 6,273; 6,327

A) 6,732; 6,327; 6,273

B) 6,273; 6,732; 6,327

C) 6,732; 6,273; 6,327

23. Round 2,156 to the nearest ten.

A) 2,150

B) 2,160

C) 2,200

21. Round 5,874 to the nearest hundred.

A) 5,800

B) 5,900

C) 5,870

24. If you round 6,349 to the nearest ten, what do you get?

A) 6,340

B) 6,350

C) 6,300

American Math Academy

1. What is 354 + 267?

A) 511

B) 621

C) 642

D) 721

2. Calculate 189 + 426.

A) 605

B) 510

C) 615

D) 510

3. Add 543, 278, and 159.

A) 920

B) 980

C) 1000

D) 1052

4. Find the sum of 726, 135, and 482.

A) 1219

B) 1343

C) 1193

D) 1443

5. What is 573 + 628?

A) 1201

B) 1210

C) 1209

D) 1301

6. Solve 387 + 214.

A) 601

B) 581

C) 704

D) 603

American Math Academy

7. Subtract 842 from 1,563.

A) 725

B) 721

C) 753

D) 721

8. Find the difference between 724 and 315.

A) 409

B) 419

C) 409

D) 410

9. What is 987 minus 468?

A) 519

B) 489

C) 509

D) 478

10. Calculate 1,234 - 567.

A) 667

B) 668

C) 777

D) 867

11. Subtract 596 from 1,825.

A) 1229

B) 1249

C) 1239

D) 1539

12. What is 2,379 minus 1,564?

A) 825

B) 811

C) 815

D) 829

American Math Academy

13. Calculate 25 × 38.

A) 940

B) 850

C) 950

D) 750

16. Find the product of 57 and 18.

A) 1036

B) 1016

C) 1026

D) 1096

14. What is 49 multiplied by 73?

A) 3591

B) 3617

C) 3577

D) 3491

17. Calculate 63 × 24.

A) 1512

B) 1572

C) 1472

D) 1542

15. Multiply 32 by 46.

A) 1522

B) 1472

C) 1512

D) 1412

18. What is 48 times 19?

A) 888

B) 868

C) 912

D) 878

American Math Academy

19. Divide 432 by 24.

A) 16

B) 18

C) 24

D) 20

22. Divide 648 by 36.

A) 18

B) 16

C) 20

D) 24

20. Find how many times 795 can be divided by 15.

A) 51

B) 53

C) 47

D) 50

23. Find the quotient of $966 \div 42$.

A) 23

B) 22

C) 24

D) 21

21. Calculate $814 \div 37$.

A) 21

B) 22

C) 23

D) 24

24. Divide 729 by 27.

A) 27

B) 25

C) 30

D) 28

American Math Academy

Mixed Review Test 3

1. What is 348 + 275?

A) 523

B) 613

C) 623

D) 625

4. Find the sum of 726, 135, and 482.

A) 1219

B) 1343

C) 1193

D) 1443

2. Calculate 189 + 426.

A) 515

B) 615

C) 620

D) 515

5. What is 573 + 628?

A) 1201

B) 1210

C) 1209

D) 1301

3. Add 543, 278, and 159.

A) 900

B) 980

C) 1000

D) 1052

6. Solve 387 + 214.

A) 601

B) 581

C) 704

D) 603

American Math Academy

AMERICAN MATH
ACADEMY

7. Subtract 842 from 1,563.

A) 725

B) 721

C) 753

D) 821

10. Calculate 1,234 - 567.

A) 667

B) 668

C) 777

D) 690

8. Find the difference between 724 and 315.

A) 409

B) 419

C) 408

D) 410

11. Subtract 596 from 1,825.

A) 1229

B) 1249

C) 1239

D) 1259

9. What is 987 minus 468?

A) 519

B) 489

C) 509

D) 478

12. What is 2,379 minus 1,564?

A) 825

B) 811

C) 815

D) 820

American Math Academy

13. Calculate 25 × 38.

A) 950

B) 960

C) 970

D) 980

16. Find the product of 57 and 18.

A) 1026

B) 1016

C) 1126

D) 1096

14. What is 49 multiplied by 73?

A) 3499

B) 3617

C) 3577

D) 3491

17. Calculate 63 × 24.

A) 1512

B) 1572

C) 1472

D) 1542

15. Multiply 32 by 46.

A) 1472

B) 1475

C) 1479

D) 1482

18. What is 48 times 19?

A) 912

B) 868

C) 798

D) 878

American Math Academy

19. Divide 432 by 24.

    A) 16

    B) 18

    C) 24

    D) 20

22. Divide 648 by 36.

    A) 18

    B) 16

    C) 20

    D) 24

20. Find how many times 795 can be divided by 15.

    A) 51

    B) 53

    C) 47

    D) 50

23. What is the value of the digit 7 in the number 7,834?

    A) 7

    B) 70

    C) 700

    D) 7,000

21. Calculate $777 \div 37$.

    A) 21

    B) 22

    C) 23

    D) 24

24. In the number 5,962, which digit is in the thousands place?

    A) 5

    B) 9

    C) 6

    D) 2

American Math Academy

25. What is the digit in the tens place in the number 3,275?

A) 3

B) 2

C) 7

D) 5

28. Compare: 5,327 ____ 5,723

A) < (less than)

B) > (greater than)

C) = (equal to)

26. In the number 8,164, which digit is in the thousands place?

A) 8

B) 1

C) 6

D) 4

29. If a number has the digit 8 in the tens place, is it greater or less than a number with 7 in the tens place?

A) Greater

B) Less

C) Equal

27. Which of the following numbers is the largest?

A) 6,482

B) 6,824

C) 8,246

D) 8,642

30. Which of the following numbers is the smallest?

A) 4,256

B) 4,562

C) 4,625

D) 4,265

American Math Academy

31. Arrange the following numbers in ascending order: 4,621; 4,216; 4,162

   A) 4,162; 4,216; 4,621

   B) 4,216; 4,162; 4,621

   C) 4,621; 4,162; 4,216

32. Put the following numbers in descending order: 7,843; 7,189; 7,421

   A) 7,843; 7,421; 7,189

   B) 7,421; 7,189; 7,843

   C) 7,843; 7,189; 7,421

33. What number comes between 3,456 and 3,458?

   A) 3,457

   B) 3,459

   C) 3,455

34. Round 6,892 to the nearest hundred.

   A) 6,900

   B) 6,800

   C) 7,000

35. If you round 9,743 to the nearest thousand, what do you get?

   A) 9,700

   B) 10,000

   C) 9,800

36. Round 3,265 to the nearest ten.

   A) 3,260

   B) 3,300

   C) 3,270

American Math Academy

1. If there are 5 boxes, and each box contains 8 pencils, how many pencils are there in total?

A) 13

B) 35

C) 40

D) 15

2. Sarah wants to buy 3 packs of stickers, and each pack has 6 stickers. How many stickers will she have in total?

A) 9

B) 12

C) 18

D) 36

3. If there are 4 bags of marbles, and each bag contains 10 marbles, how many marbles are there in total?

A) 20

B) 30

C) 40

D) 100

4. What is the estimated product of 25 and 8?

A) 30

B) 200

C) 250

D) 40

5. If you round 6.78 to the nearest whole number and multiply it by 5, what is the estimated product?

A) 30

B) 40

C) 35

D) 45

6. Estimate the product of 7 and 9.

A) 56

B) 70

C) 63

D) 50

American Math Academy

7. Use the distributive property to simplify:
$4 \times (7 + 3)$

A) 47

B) 34

C) 40

D) 31

8. If you distribute 5 in the expression $5 \times (8 - 2)$, what is the result?

A) 40

B) 25

C) 50

D) 30

9. Simplify: $3 \times (12 - 5)$ using the distributive property.

A) 31

B) 49

C) 21

D) 27

10. What are the factors of 24?

A) 1, 2, 3, 4, 6, 12, 24

B) 2, 6, 12

C) 4, 8

D) 3, 9

11. Find the factors of 15.

A) 1, 15

B) 2, 3, 5

C) 4, 8

D) 1, 3, 5, 15

12. What are the factors of 18?

A) 1, 18

B) 2, 3, 6, 9

C) 1, 2, 3, 6, 9, 18

D) 5, 10

American Math Academy

13. If there are 6 bags of candies, and each bag contains 9 candies, how many candies are there in total?

A) 15

B) 45

C) 54

D) 69

16. What is the estimated product of 38 and 7?

A) 14

B) 280

C) 308

D) 56

14. Jenny wants to distribute 4 boxes of crayons, and each box contains 12 crayons. How many crayons will she distribute?

A) 8

B) 12

C) 16

D) 48

17. If you round 9.25 to the nearest whole number and multiply it by 6, what is the estimated product?

A) 6

B) 50

C) 60

D) 54

15. There are 5 jars of jam, and each jar holds 15 ounces. How many ounces of jam are there in total?

A) 20

B) 50

C) 75

D) 100

18. Estimate the product of 8 and 11.

A) 64

B) 80

C) 88

D) 48

American Math Academy

19. Use the distributive property to simplify:
$3 \times (10 + 2)$

A) 32

B) 36

C) 30

D) 26

20. If you distribute 4 in the expression $4 \times (9 - 3)$, what is the result?

A) 4

B) 24

C) 36

D) 12

21. Simplify: $2 \times (15 - 7)$ using the distributive property.

A) 22

B) 16

C) 28

D) 30

22. What are the factors of 36?

A) 1, 36

B) 2, 6, 12, 18

C) 4, 8, 16, 32

D) 1, 2, 3, 4, 6, 9, 12, 18, 36

23. Find the factors of 21.

A) 1, 21

B) 1, 3, 7, 21

C) 4, 8

D) 5, 10

24. What are the factors of 48?

A) 1, 48

B) 2, 3, 4, 6, 8, 12, 16, 24

C) 5, 10

D) 1, 2, 3, 4, 6, 8, 12, 16, 24, 48

American Math Academy

Mixed Review Test 5

1. Is 7 a prime number or a composite number?

A) Prime

B) Composite

C) Neither

2. What is the only even prime number?

A) 2

B) 4

C) 6

D) 8

3. Which of the following numbers is a composite number?

A) 11

B) 17

C) 15

D) 13

4. Is 1 a prime number or a composite number?

A) Prime

B) Composite

C) Neither

5. What is the next number in the pattern: 5, 9, 13, 17, __?

A) 20

B) 21

C) 18

D) 22

6. Find the missing number in the subtraction pattern: 36 - 12, 30 - 6, 24 - __.

A) 18

B) 14

C) 9

D) 0

American Math Academy

AMERICAN MATH
ACADEMY

7. If you add 8 to the previous number each time, what is the next number in the pattern: 3, 11, 19, __?

A) 27

B) 32

C) 36

D) 42

10. Find the missing number in the division pattern: 49 ÷ 7, 42 ÷ 6, 35 ÷ __.

A) 4

B) 5

C) 7

D) 8

8. What is the next number in the pattern: 100, 90, 80, 70, __?

A) 65

B) 60

C) 55

D) 50

11. If you multiply by 5 each time, what is the next number in the pattern: 2, 10, 50, __?

A) 250

B) 100

C) 75

D) 25

9. What is the next number in the pattern: 4, 12, 36, 108, __?

A) 216

B) 324

C) 342

D) 348

12. What is the next number in the pattern: 64, 32, 16, 8, __?

A) 6

B) 4

C) 12

D) 2

American Math Academy

13. What type of fraction is $\frac{5}{7}$?

A) Proper fraction

B) Improper fraction

C) Mixed number

16. What is a fraction with a numerator of 1 called?

A) Whole number

B) Unit fraction

C) Mixed number

14. If the numerator is greater than or equal to the denominator, it is a:

A) Proper fraction

B) Improper fraction

C) Mixed number

17. Which of these fractions is equivalent to $\frac{2}{3}$?

A) $\frac{4}{6}$

B) $\frac{5}{7}$

C) $\frac{3}{5}$

15. Which of the following fractions is a mixed number?

A) $\frac{5}{4}$

B) $\frac{9}{2}$

C) $\frac{3}{7}$

18. Reduce $\frac{4}{8}$ to its simplest form. What is the simplified fraction?

A) $\frac{1}{8}$

B) $\frac{2}{3}$

C) $\frac{1}{2}$

American Math Academy

19. What is the equivalent fraction of $\frac{3}{4}$ with a denominator of 12?

A) $\frac{9}{12}$

B) $\frac{2}{3}$

C) $\frac{6}{9}$

22. What is the next number in the pattern: 14, 24, 34, 44, __?

A) 45

B) 54

C) 64

D) 74

20. Simplify $\frac{10}{15}$ to its simplest form. What is the simplified fraction?

A) $\frac{5}{10}$

B) $\frac{2}{3}$

C) $\frac{1}{2}$

23. What is the next number in the pattern: 5, 10, 20, 40, __?

A) 60

B) 80

C) 100

D) 120

21. Is 29 a prime number or a composite number?

A) Prime

B) Composite

C) Neither

24. Which fraction is equivalent to $\frac{3}{5}$?

A) $\frac{4}{7}$

B) $\frac{6}{10}$

C) $\frac{2}{3}$

American Math Academy

1. Which fraction is larger: $\frac{2}{5}$ or $\frac{3}{7}$?

A) $\frac{2}{5}$

B) $\frac{3}{7}$

C) They are equal

2. Compare $\frac{4}{8}$ and $\frac{3}{6}$. Which fraction is larger?

A) $\frac{4}{8}$

B) $\frac{3}{6}$

C) They are equal

3. What is greater, $\frac{5}{9}$ or $\frac{4}{7}$?

A) $\frac{5}{9}$

B) $\frac{4}{7}$

C) They are equal

4. Which fraction is smaller: $\frac{1}{6}$ or $\frac{2}{9}$?

A) $\frac{1}{6}$

B) $\frac{2}{9}$

C) They are equal

5. Arrange these fractions in ascending order: $\frac{2}{5}, \frac{1}{4}, \frac{3}{6}$.

A) $\frac{1}{4}, \frac{2}{5}, \frac{3}{6}$

B) $\frac{3}{6}, \frac{1}{4}, \frac{2}{5}$

C) $\frac{3}{6}, \frac{2}{5}, \frac{1}{4}$

6. Put these fractions in descending order: $\frac{4}{7}, \frac{5}{9}, \frac{3}{8}$.

A) $\frac{5}{9}, \frac{4}{7}, \frac{3}{8}$

B) $\frac{4}{7}, \frac{5}{9}, \frac{3}{8}$

C) $\frac{5}{9}, \frac{3}{8}, \frac{4}{7}$

American Math Academy

AMERICAN MATH
ACADEMY

7. What is $\frac{1}{4} + \frac{2}{4}$?

A) $\frac{3}{4}$

B) $\frac{1}{8}$

C) $\frac{3}{2}$

D) $\frac{1}{2}$

8. Subtract $\frac{5}{6}$ from $\frac{3}{6}$.

A) $\frac{2}{6}$

B) $\frac{1}{6}$

C) $\frac{4}{6}$

D) $\frac{3}{12}$

9. If Sarah ate $\frac{3}{4}$ of a pizza, how much is left?

A) $\frac{1}{4}$

B) $\frac{1}{2}$

C) $\frac{1}{3}$

D) $\frac{2}{3}$

10. Mary had $\frac{2}{5}$ of a chocolate bar. She gave $\frac{1}{10}$ of it to her friend. How much of the chocolate bar does she have left?

A) $\frac{2}{10}$

B) $\frac{3}{10}$

C) $\frac{1}{5}$

D) $\frac{1}{2}$

11. If a rope is cut into 6 equal pieces, and 4 pieces are used, what fraction of the rope is left?

A) $\frac{1}{3}$

B) $\frac{1}{4}$

C) $\frac{1}{6}$

D) $\frac{3}{6}$

12. A recipe calls for $\frac{2}{4}$ cup of flour, and you have already used $\frac{1}{4}$ cup. How much more flour is needed?

A) $\frac{1}{2}$ cup

B) $\frac{1}{3}$ cup

C) $\frac{1}{4}$ cup

D) $\frac{3}{4}$ cup

American Math Academy

13. Which fraction is greater: $\frac{5}{8}$ or $\frac{4}{9}$?

    A) $\frac{5}{8}$

    B) $\frac{4}{9}$

    C) They are equal

14. Compare $\frac{3}{7}$ and $\frac{2}{5}$. Which fraction is larger?

    A) $\frac{3}{7}$

    B) $\frac{2}{5}$

    C) They are equal

15. Arrange these fractions in ascending order: $\frac{2}{3}, \frac{5}{6}, \frac{3}{4}$.

    A) $\frac{2}{3}, \frac{5}{6}, \frac{3}{4}$

    B) $\frac{3}{4}, \frac{5}{6}, \frac{2}{3}$

    C) $\frac{5}{6}, \frac{3}{4}, \frac{2}{3}$

16. Put these fractions in descending order: $\frac{7}{8}, \frac{1}{4}, \frac{5}{6}$.

    A) $\frac{7}{8}, \frac{5}{6}, \frac{1}{4}$

    B) $\frac{5}{6}, \frac{7}{8}, \frac{1}{4}$

    C) $\frac{7}{8}, \frac{1}{4}, \frac{5}{6}$

17. What is $\frac{3}{5} + \frac{2}{5}$?

    A) $\frac{5}{5}$

    B) $\frac{4}{5}$

    C) $\frac{1}{10}$

    D) $\frac{5}{10}$

18. Subtract $\frac{4}{9}$ from $\frac{7}{9}$.

    A) $\frac{1}{9}$

    B) $\frac{3}{9}$

    C) $\frac{2}{9}$

    D) $\frac{1}{18}$

American Math Academy

AMERICAN MATH ACADEMY

19. If Susan baked a cake and ate $\frac{3}{8}$ of it, how much of the cake is left?

A) $\frac{1}{2}$

B) $\frac{5}{8}$

C) $\frac{1}{4}$

D) $\frac{3}{4}$

20. There were $\frac{5}{6}$ of a pizza left. John ate $\frac{2}{3}$ of what was left. How much of the pizza did John eat?

A) $\frac{1}{6}$

B) $\frac{2}{9}$

C) $\frac{1}{3}$

D) $\frac{4}{9}$

21. If a ribbon is $\frac{1}{3}$ yard long, and you cut off $\frac{1}{4}$ of it, how long is the piece you cut off?

A) $\frac{1}{7}$ yard

B) $\frac{2}{12}$ yard

C) $\frac{1}{12}$ yard

D) $\frac{2}{7}$ yard

22. A recipe calls for $\frac{3}{5}$ cup of sugar, but you only have $\frac{2}{5}$ cup. How much more sugar do you need?

A) $\frac{3}{5}$ cup

B) $\frac{1}{10}$ cup

C) $\frac{1}{5}$ cup

D) $\frac{1}{2}$ cup

23. Compare $\frac{1}{2}$ and $\frac{2}{4}$. Which fraction is larger?

A) $\frac{1}{2}$

B) $\frac{2}{4}$

C) They are equal

24. What is $\frac{5}{6} - \frac{1}{6}$?

A) $\frac{4}{6}$

B) $\frac{6}{6}$

C) $\frac{1}{6}$

D) $\frac{4}{12}$

American Math Academy

1 What is the decimal equivalent of $\frac{3}{4}$?

A) 0.25

B) 0.5

C) 0.75

D) 1.25

4 Convert 0.6 to a fraction in its simplest form.

A) $\frac{3}{5}$

B) $\frac{6}{10}$

C) $\frac{60}{100}$

D) $\frac{1}{6}$

2 Express 2.5 as a fraction in its simplest form.

A) $\frac{5}{2}$

B) $\frac{2}{5}$

C) $\frac{25}{15}$

D) $\frac{1}{4}$

5. Which is greater: 0.79 or 0.97?

A) 0.79

B) 0.97

C) They are equal

3 Which of the following is a mixed number?

A) 0.25

B) 0.75

C) $1\frac{1}{4}$

D) $\frac{1}{4}$

6. Compare 0.6 and 0.06. Which decimal is larger?

A) 0.6

B) 0.06

C) They are equal

American Math Academy

7. How many centimeters are in 2 meters?

A) 20

B) 200

C) 2,000

D) 200,000

10. Convert 3 feet to yards.

A) 1

B) 2

C) 3

D) 4

8. Convert 5 kilometers to meters.

A) 500

B) 5,000

C) 50,000

D) 500,000

11. How many minutes are in 2 hours?

A) 30

B) 60

C) 90

D) 120

9. How many inches are in a foot?

A) 6

B) 10

C) 12

D) 24

12. Convert 45 minutes to hours.

A) 0.45

B) 0.75

C) 1.25

D) 0.25

American Math Academy

13. What is the decimal equivalent of $\frac{1}{3}$?

A) 0.3

B) 0.33

C) 0.3333...

D) 0.5

14. Express 0.75 as a fraction in its simplest form.

A) $\frac{3}{4}$

B) $\frac{3}{5}$

C) $\frac{7}{5}$

D) $\frac{75}{100}$

15. Which of the following is a terminating decimal?

A) 0.125

B) 0.333...

C) 0.75

D) 1.25

16. Convert 2.25 to a fraction in its simplest form.

A) $\frac{9}{4}$

B) $\frac{225}{100}$

C) $2\frac{1}{4}$

D) $\frac{225}{200}$

17. Which is greater: 0.89 or 0.98?

A) 0.89

B) 0.98

C) They are equal

18. Compare 0.45 and 0.045. Which decimal is larger?

A) 0.45

B) 0.045

C) They are equal

19. How many millimeters are in 3 centimeters?

A) 0.3

B) 3

C) 30

D) 300

20. Convert 4 kilometers to meters.

A) 4,000

B) 40,000

C) 400,000

D) 4,000,000

21. How many ounces are in a pound?

A) 8

B) 12

C) 16

D) 32

22. Convert 2 quarts to pints.

A) 1

B) 2

C) 3

D) 4

23. How many seconds are in 3 minutes?

A) 30

B) 60

C) 90

D) 180

24. Convert 2.5 hours to minutes.

A) 25

B) 75

C) 150

D) 250

American Math Academy

Mixed Review Test 8

1. What is the measure of a right angle?

A) 45 degrees

B) 90 degrees

C) 135 degrees

D) 180 degrees

2. An acute angle measures:

A) Less than 90 degrees

B) Exactly 90 degrees

C) Between 90 and 180 degrees

D) More than 180 degrees

3. A straight angle measures:

A) Less than 90 degrees

B) Exactly 90 degrees

C) 180 degrees

D) More than 180 degrees

4. An obtuse angle measures:

A) Less than 90 degrees

B) Exactly 90 degrees

C) Between 90 and 180 degrees

D) More than 180 degrees

5. What type of angle is formed when two angles add up to 90 degrees?

A) Acute angle

B) Right angle

C) Obtuse angle

D) Straight angle

6. If an angle measures 120 degrees, what type of angle is it?

A) Acute angle

B) Right angle

C) Obtuse angle

D) Straight angle

American Math Academy

AMERICAN MATH
ACADEMY

7. A shape with four equal sides and four right angles is called a:

A) Square

B) Rectangle

C) Parallelogram

D) Rhombus

8. What type of quadrilateral has one pair of opposite sides that are parallel?

A) Square

B) Rectangle

C) Parallelogram

D) Rhombus

9. A shape with equal sides and no right angles is called a:

A) Square

B) Rectangle

C) Parallelogram

D) Rhombus

10 What is the measure of an obtuse angle?

A) Less than 90 degrees

B) Exactly 90 degrees

C) Between 90 and 180 degrees

D) More than 180 degrees

11 How many degrees are in a straight angle?

A) 45 degrees

B) 90 degrees

C) 135 degrees

D) 180 degrees

12 An angle that is less than 90 degrees and greater than 0 degrees is called:

A) Acute angle

B) Right angle

C) Obtuse angle

D) Straight angle

American Math Academy

13 If an angle measures 60 degrees, what type of angle is it?

A) Acute angle

B) Right angle

C) Obtuse angle

D) Straight angle

16 A shape with four sides of equal length and four right angles is called a:

A) Square

B) Rectangle

C) Parallelogram

D) Trapezoid

14 What type of angle is formed when two angles add up to 180 degrees?

A) Acute angle

B) Right angle

C) Obtuse angle

D) Straight angle

17 What type of quadrilateral has one pair of opposite sides that are equal in length?

A) Square

B) Rectangle

C) Parallelogram

D) Rhombus

15 If an angle measures 90 degrees, it is called:

A) Acute angle

B) Right angle

C) Obtuse angle

D) Straight angle

18 A shape with no right angles is called a:

A) Square

B) Rectangle

C) Parallelogram

D) Rhombus

American Math Academy

Mixed Review Test 9

1. What is the perimeter of a rectangle with a length of 8 meters and a width of 5 meters?

A) 10 meters

B) 13 meters

C) 26 meters

D) 40 meters

2. If a square has sides of length 7 centimeters, what is its perimeter?

A) 7 centimeters

B) 14 centimeters

C) 21 centimeters

D) 28 centimeters

3. A triangle has sides measuring 6 inches, 8 inches, and 10 inches. What is its perimeter?

A) 6 inches

B) 20 inches

C) 24 inches

D) 48 inches

4. Find the perimeter of a regular hexagon with each side measuring 5 inches.

A) 5 inches

B) 10 inches

C) 20 inches

D) 30 inches

5. A garden is in the shape of a pentagon, and each side measures 12 feet. What is the perimeter of the garden?

A) 12 feet

B) 24 feet

C) 60 feet

D) 120 feet

6. What is the area of a square with sides of length 6 centimeters?

A) 6 square centimeters

B) 12 square centimeters

C) 24 square centimeters

D) 36 square centimeters

American Math Academy

7. Calculate the area of a rectangle with a length of 9 meters and a width of 4 meters.

A) 9 square meters

B) 13.5 square meters

C) 36 square meters

D) 72 square meters

8. A triangle has a base of 7 inches and a height of 9 inches. What is its area?

A) 9 square inches

B) 31.5 square inches

C) 63 square inches

D) 126 square inches

9. Determine the area of a parallelogram with a base of 6 meters and a height of 8 meters.

A) 6 square meters

B) 12 square meters

C) 48 square meters

D) 72 square meters

10. The area of a circle with a radius of 5 centimeters is approximately: $\pi = 3 \cdot 14$

A) 15.7 square centimeters

B) 25 square centimeters

C) 31.4 square centimeters

D) 78.5 square centimeters

11. If a rectangle has a length of 12 centimeters and a width of 3 centimeters, what is its perimeter?

A) 15 centimeters

B) 18 centimeters

C) 24 centimeters

D) 30 centimeters

12. Find the perimeter of a regular octagon with each side measuring 9 inches.

A) 9 inches

B) 18 inches

C) 45 inches

D) 72 inches

American Math Academy

13. A playground is in the shape of a heptagon, and each side measures 15 feet. What is the perimeter of the playground?

A) 15 feet

B) 30 feet

C) 75 feet

D) 105 feet

16. Calculate the area of a rectangle with a length of 10 inches and a width of 5 inches.

A) 10 square inches

B) 15 square inches

C) 25 square inches

D) 50 square inches

14. A triangle has sides measuring 12 centimeters, 15 centimeters, and 20 centimeters. What is its perimeter?

A) 12 centimeters

B) 30 centimeters

C) 47 centimeters

D) 80 centimeters

17. A triangle has a base of 8 feet and a height of 6 feet. What is its area?

A) 12 square feet

B) 20 square feet

C) 24 square feet

D) 48 square feet

15. What is the area of a square with sides of length 9 meters?

A) 9 square meters

B) 18 square meters

C) 27 square meters

D) 81 square meters

18. Determine the area of a parallelogram with a base of 12 meters and a height of 7 meters.

A) 7 square meters

B) 12 square meters

C) 84 square meters

D) 168 square meters

American Math Academy

19. The area of a circle with a radius of 6 centimeters is approximately: $\pi = 3 \cdot 14$

A) 18.84 square centimeters

B) 36 square centimeters

C) 113.04 square centimeters

D) 226.08 square centimeters

22. A rectangular garden measures 15 meters in length and 8 meters in width. What is its perimeter?

A) 15 meters

B) 23 meters

C) 46 meters

D) 61 meters

20. What is the area of a rhombus with diagonals of length 10 inches and 12 inches?

A) 60 square inches

B) 120 square inches

C) 180 square inches

D) 240 square inches

23. Calculate the area of a circle with a radius of 10 centimeters. $\pi = 3 \cdot 14$

A) 31.4 square centimeters

B) 62.8 square centimeters

C) 100 square centimeters

D) 314 square centimeters

American Math Academy

21. What is the perimeter of a regular pentagon with each side measuring 6 inches?

A) 6 inches

B) 12 inches

C) 18 inches

D) 30 inches

24. The area of a triangle with a base of 6 meters and a height of 9 meters is:

A) 18 square meters

B) 27 square meters

C) 36 square meters

D) 54 square meters

Mixed Review Test 10

1. What is the sum of 387 and 249?

A) 536

B) 636

C) 736

D) 836

2. If you subtract 548 from 942, what is the result?

A) 394

B) 348

C) 94

D) 384

3. What is 24 multiplied by 17?

A) 408

B) 412

C) 516

D) 720

4. If you divide 918 by 6, what is the quotient?

A) 138

B) 153

C) 162

D) 276

5. In the number 5,379, which digit is in the hundreds place?

A) 5

B) 3

C) 7

D) 9

6. What is the value of the digit 8 in the number 6,874?

A) 800

B) 80

C) 8

D) 8000

American Math Academy

7. Which number is the largest among these: 4,329, 4,239, 4,932, 4,392?

A) 4,329

B) 4,239

C) 4,932

D) 4,392

10. If you round 3,265 to the nearest ten, what is the result?

A) 3,260

B) 3,270

C) 3,300

D) 3,200

8. Arrange these numbers in descending order: 726, 917, 543, 862.

A) 726, 917, 543, 862

B) 917, 726, 862, 543

C) 917, 862, 726, 543

D) 726, 862, 543, 917

11. Is the number 29 prime or composite?

A) Prime

B) Composite

9. Round 6,843 to the nearest hundred.

A) 6,800

B) 6,840

C) 6,900

D) 7,000

12. Which of the following numbers is a composite number: 17, 24, 31, 41?

A) 17

B) 24

C) 31

D) 41

American Math Academy

13. What comes next in the pattern: 5, 10, 15, 20, __?

A) 25

B) 30

C) 35

D) 40

14. If you subtract 5 from the previous number of 35, what is the result?

A) 25

B) 30

C) 35

D) 40

15. If you multiply 3 by 17, what is the result?

A) 18

B) 21

C) 31

D) 51

16. If you divide 12 by 3, what is the quotient?

A) 4

B) 6

C) 9

D) 3

17. Which fraction is larger: $\frac{2}{5}$ or $\frac{3}{7}$?

A) $\frac{2}{5}$

B) $\frac{3}{7}$

18. If you compare $\frac{4}{9}$ and $\frac{5}{12}$, which fraction is smaller?

A) $\frac{4}{9}$

B) $\frac{5}{12}$

American Math Academy

19. Arrange these fractions in ascending order: $\frac{1}{3}, \frac{2}{5}, \frac{4}{7}, \frac{3}{8}$.

A) $\frac{1}{3}, \frac{2}{5}, \frac{4}{7}, \frac{3}{8}$

B) $\frac{1}{3}, \frac{3}{8}, \frac{2}{5}, \frac{4}{7}$

C) $\frac{3}{8}, \frac{1}{3}, \frac{4}{7}, \frac{2}{5}$

D) $\frac{2}{5}, \frac{1}{3}, \frac{3}{8}, \frac{4}{7}$

21. What is the result of adding $\frac{1}{4}$ and $\frac{2}{7}$?

A) $\frac{3}{4}$

B) $\frac{9}{28}$

C) $\frac{6}{7}$

D) $\frac{15}{28}$

20. What is the largest fraction among these: $\frac{5}{9}$, $\frac{3}{7}, \frac{2}{5}, \frac{4}{11}$?

A) $\frac{5}{9}$

B) $\frac{3}{7}$

C) $\frac{2}{5}$

D) $\frac{4}{11}$

22. If you subtract $\frac{3}{8}$ from $\frac{1}{2}$, what is the result?

A) $\frac{5}{8}$

B) $\frac{1}{8}$

C) $\frac{1}{3}$

D) $\frac{4}{8}$

American Math Academy

AMERICAN MATH
ACADEMY

23. If you have $\frac{3}{4}$ of a pizza, and you eat $\frac{1}{8}$ of it, how much is left?

A) $\frac{5}{8}$

B) $\frac{1}{8}$

C) $\frac{3}{4}$

D) $\frac{7}{8}$

25. What is the result of adding $\frac{3}{5}$ and $\frac{1}{3}$?

A) $\frac{14}{15}$

B) $\frac{6}{15}$

C) $\frac{8}{15}$

D) $\frac{12}{15}$

24. Sarah has $\frac{2}{3}$ of a chocolate bar, and she gives $\frac{1}{4}$ of it to her friend. What fraction of the chocolate bar is left?

A) $\frac{1}{6}$

B) $\frac{1}{4}$

C) $\frac{1}{3}$

D) $\frac{5}{12}$

26. If you subtract $\frac{2}{7}$ from $\frac{4}{9}$, what is the result?

A) $\frac{1}{7}$

B) $\frac{2}{7}$

C) $\frac{10}{63}$

D) $\frac{14}{63}$

American Math Academy

27. Mary had $\frac{3}{8}$ of a pie, and she ate $\frac{1}{4}$ of it. What fraction of the pie is left?

A) $\frac{3}{32}$

B) $\frac{1}{8}$

C) $\frac{1}{4}$

D) $\frac{5}{32}$

29. Is the number 37 prime or composite?

A) Prime

B) Composite

28. If you have a cake, and you eat $\frac{2}{5}$ of it, what fraction of the cake is left?

A) $\frac{3}{5}$

B) $\frac{2}{5}$

C) $\frac{1}{5}$

D) $\frac{3}{2}$

30. Which of the following numbers is a prime number: 12, 17, 22, 33?

A) 12

B) 17

C) 22

D) 33

American Math Academy

AMERICAN MATH
ACADEMY

31. What comes next in the pattern: 8, 12, 16, 20, __?

A) 22

B) 24

C) 25

D) 28

32. If you add 5 to the previous number of 17, what is the result?

A) 22

B) 24

C) 25

D) 28

33. Which number is the smallest among these: 3,857, 3,725, 3,963, 3,683?

A) 3,857

B) 3,725

C) 3,963

D) 3,683

34. Arrange these numbers in ascending order: 5,612, 4,759, 6,321, 5,193.

A) 5,612, 4,759, 6,321, 5,193

B) 4,759, 5,193, 5,612, 6,321

C) 4,759, 5,612, 5,193, 6,321

D) 5,193, 4,759, 5,612, 6,32

American Math Academy

1. Find the area of following shape?

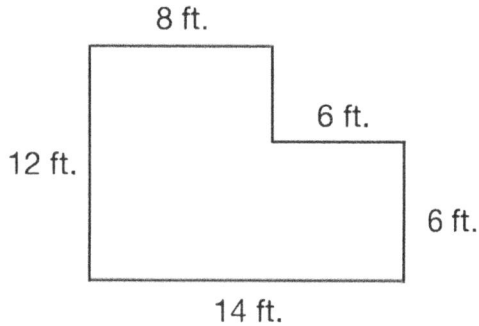

8 ft.

6 ft.

12 ft.

6 ft.

14 ft.

A) 102 ft.^{2}

B) 112 ft.^{2}

C) 122 ft.^{2}

D) 132 ft.^{2}

3. Find the perimeter of rectangular?

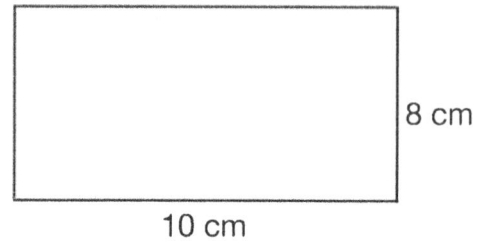

8 cm

10 cm

A) 18 m

B) 27 m

C) 36 m

D) 48 m

2. Write the measure of combined angle?

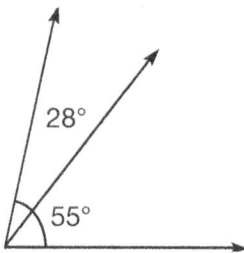

28°

55°

A) 80°

B) 82°

C) 83°

D) 85°

4. Find how many cube are in box below?

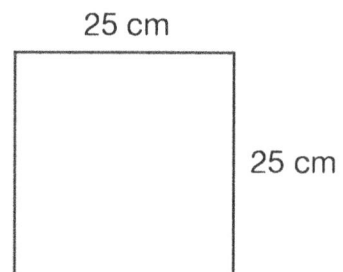

25 cm

25 cm

A) 225 cm^2

B) 250 cm^2

C) 500 cm^2

D) 625 cm^2

AMERICAN MATH
ACADEMY

5. Which of the following number sentences is a correct match with the following sentence:

18 more than the product of 3 and 4

A) $18 + 3 \times 4$

B) $18 - 3 \times 4$

C) $3 + 18 \times 4$

D) $4 + 3 \times 18$

8. What is the least common multiple of 5 and 30?

A) 5

B) 30

C) 120

D) 150

6. Add $3\frac{2}{7} + 1\frac{6}{7} = ?$

A) $2\frac{1}{7}$

B) $3\frac{1}{7}$

C) $4\frac{1}{7}$

D) $5\frac{1}{7}$

9. Subtract $12\frac{3}{5} - 3\frac{2}{5} = ?$

A) $1\frac{1}{5}$

B) $2\frac{2}{5}$

C) $6\frac{1}{5}$

D) $9\frac{1}{5}$

7. What is the least common multiple of 9 and 11?

A) 9

B) 11

C) 88

D) 99

10. What are all the factors of 35?

A) 1, 2, 3, 5, 35

B) 0, 2, 5, 15, 35

C) 1, 5, 7, 35

D) 1, 3, 7, 35

11. Solve: $8 \times 5 - 9$.

A) 13

B) 21

C) 31

D) 41

12. Vera had $55 in her bank account. She spent $24 of her dollars. How many dollars does she have left in her bank account?

A) $31

B) $34

C) $41

D) $51

13. Which of following is the same length as 100m?

A) 0.1km

B) 1km

C) 10km

D) 100km

14. Which of following measurement of length is greatest?

A) 1m

B) 1cm

C) 100mm

D) 1km

15. _____ Liters = 5,000mL

A) 0.5

B) 5

C) 50

D) 500

16. 2 years = _____ days

A) 365

B) 730

C) 1,095

D) 1,825

17. 10 gallons = _____ quarts

A) 10

B) 20

C) 30

D) 40

18. Find $\dfrac{6}{5} \times \dfrac{4}{7} = ?$

A) $\dfrac{12}{35}$

B) $\dfrac{24}{35}$

C) $\dfrac{9}{35}$

D) $\dfrac{42}{20}$

19. Vera and Nora were told to find the product $6 \times \dfrac{1}{5}$.

Vera $\rightarrow 6 \times \dfrac{1}{5} = \dfrac{1}{30}$

Nora $\rightarrow 6 \times \dfrac{1}{5} = \dfrac{6}{5}$

Which student wrote the product correctly?

A) Vera

B) Nora

C) Vera and Nora

D) None

20. Find the area of rectangular?

A) 3 in.^{2}

B) 6 in.^{2}

C) $\dfrac{3}{2}$ in.^{2}

D) $\dfrac{9}{2}$ in.^{2}

3 in.

$1\dfrac{1}{2}$ in.

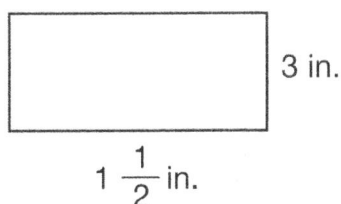

21. Vera studied her homework $\dfrac{1}{5}$ hours and Nora studied her homework $\dfrac{2}{3}$ as long as Vera. How long did Nora study?

A) $\dfrac{2}{5}$

B) $\dfrac{3}{10}$

C) $\dfrac{2}{15}$

D) $\dfrac{9}{20}$

22. Which of the following is equal to $5(4 \times 3 - 4) + 14$?

A) 14

B) 24

C) 44

D) 54

23. Which of following algebraic equations correctly represents this sentence:

Sixty – five is four times a number, increased by nine.

A) $65 = 4x - 9$

B) $65 = 4x + 9$

C) $9 = 4x - 65$

D) $9 = 4x + 65$

24. Which fraction is **not** equivalent to $\frac{3}{4}$?

A) $\frac{9}{12}$

B) $\frac{15}{20}$

C) $\frac{5}{20}$

D) $\frac{18}{24}$

25. Find $\frac{1}{2} \times \frac{3}{5}$.

A) $\frac{1}{2}$

B) $\frac{3}{5}$

C) $\frac{3}{10}$

D) $\frac{3}{15}$

26. Find $\frac{3}{5} + \frac{9}{3}$.

A) $3\frac{3}{5}$

B) $1\frac{1}{5}$

C) $2\frac{3}{5}$

D) $2\frac{2}{5}$

27. Find $\frac{7}{27} - \frac{1}{27}$.

A) $\frac{1}{3}$

B) $\frac{2}{9}$

C) 3

D) 9

28. What is the sum of 5 and $3\frac{1}{2}$?

A) $\frac{2}{17}$

B) $3\frac{1}{2}$

C) $5\frac{1}{2}$

D) $8\frac{1}{2}$

29. If Vera ate $\frac{1}{3}$ of apple and her friend Nora ate $\frac{1}{3}$ of apple. How much of the apple remains?

A) 1

B) 2

C) $\frac{1}{2}$

D) $\frac{1}{3}$

30. What is 665 − 178?

A) 487

B) 547

C) 647

D) 747

33. What is the product of 15 and 75?

A) 125

B) 1,105

C) 1,120

D) 1,125

31. What is 3,745 + 328?

A) 473

B) 4,073

C) 40,730

D) 400,730

34. What is the sum of 567 and 236?

A) 700

B) 800

C) 803

D) 805

32. What is $4\overline{)168}$

A) 21

B) 42

C) 52

D) 64

35. Find 995 ÷ 5 = ?

A) 1.99

B) 19.9

C) 199

D) 199.9

36. Which of following expression is equivalent to 100,000?

A) 10^3

B) 10^4

C) 10^5

D) 10^6

39. $147 \times 12 =$ _____

A) 1,700

B) 1,760

C) 1,764

D) 1,864

37. Add   415
     + 408
     _____

A) 403

B) 483

C) 503

D) 823

40. 92 – 33 which of following addition prob - lem could we use to check our answer?

A) 92 + 33

B) 33 + 43

C) 33 + 59

D) 59 + 59

38. Subtract   167
        – 89
        _____

A) 58

B) 68

C) 78

D) 98

41. What is 213×11?

A) 233

B) 2.340

C) 2,343

D) 2,543

42. Solve 728
            − 499

A) 209

B) 219

C) 229

D) 239

45. Which of following expression is the same as 8 × 1000?

A) 8

B) 80

C) 800

D) 8,000

43. Solve 325
            ×   6

A) 256

B) 1,950

C) 2,136

D) 3,356

46. Which of following expression is the same as 1.4 × 100 ?

A) 14

B) 140

C) 1,400

D) 14,000

44. Which number is the product of 425 and 10?

A) 425

B) 4,250

C) 42,500

D) 425,000

47. Which of following expression is the same as 1.6 × 10 ?

A) 16

B) 160

C) 1600

D) 16,000

48. What digit is in hundred place in 1,578?

A) 4

B) 5

C) 7

D) 8

51. Which of following decimal has the greatest value?

A) 26.45

B) 26.54

C) 26.60

D) 26.46

49. What digit is in ten place in 312?

A) 1

B) 2

C) 3

D) 5

52. Which number rounds to 35,000?

A) 33,99

B) 34,098

C) 34,890

D) 35,987

53. Round the whole number to the given place. 6,368 to the nearest thousand.

50. What is the value of 6 in 3,046?

A) 6

B) 60

C) 600

D) 6000

A) 4,000

B) 500

C) 6,000

D) 7,000

MATH WORKBOOK GRADE 4

ANSWER KEY

Pretest

1	2	3	4	5	6	7	8	9	10	11	12	13	14	15
C	B	B	B	D	C	B	D	A	B	B	C	D	B	D

16	17	18	19	20	21
B	A	C	C	D	D

Worksheet 1

1
9,000,000 + 200,000 + 30,000 + 4,000 + 400 + 50 + 6

2	3
7,000,000 + 800,000 + 90,000 + 1,000 + 300 + 40 + 5	800,000 + 40,000 + 5,000 + 600 + 10 + 2

4	5	6	7	8
50,000 + 6,000 + 10 + 7	6,000 + 900 + 10 + 7	200 + 90 + 1	30 + 1	50,000 + 6,000 + 200

9	10
6,000 + 900 + 1	50,000 + 800 + 30 + 6

Worksheet 2

1	2	3	4	5	6
6,798,914	667,952	9,698,734	87,953	9,498	56,482,345

7	8	9	10	11
9,689,731	4,643	919	8,465	461

Worksheet 3

1

Seven million seven hundred thirty five thousand and s hundred fourth-five

2

Seven hundred eighty five thousand and six hundred twenty-five

3

Thirty five thousand and five hundred seventy eight

4

Five thousand and nine hundred seventy four

5

Siz hundred seventy eight

6

Three thousand and three hundred thirty three

7

Four thousand and four hundred twenty nine

8

Sixty seven thousand and one hundred ninety two

9

Three hundred sixty seven thousand and five hundred seventy four

10

Three tousand and six hundred fourth nine

Worksheet 4

1	2	3	4	5	6	7	8	9	10	11	12	13	14	15
<	<	>	<	>	<	>	<	<	<	=	=	<	>	<

16	17	18
<	<	>

Worksheet 5

1	**2**	**3**
165<325<986	7,776<8,962<13,520	365<650<750
4	**5**	**6**
4,444<5,555<6,666	4,980<7,456<12,350	13,300<13,450<13,500
7	**8**	**9**
11,380<11,470<11,490	16,770<16,792<16,795	18<950<20,054<20,154
10	**11**	**12**
968<9,875<10,750	3,678<7,765<15,384	9,128<12,368<77,998
13	**14**	
19,161<10,166<10,189	5,468<5,486<5,488	

Worksheet 6

1	**2**	**3**	**4**	**5**
7,000,000	35,000,000	503,100	7,000	2,000,000
6	**7**	**8**	**9**	**10**
380	456,300	1,230	3,548,000	12,000,000
11	**12**	**13**	**14**	**15**
130	70	800	900	1,400
16	**17**	**18**		
697,370	3,390	13,000		

Worksheet 7

1	2	3	4	5	6
3,000	8,000	5,000	9,000	8,000	13,000

7	8	9	10	11	12
17,000	18,000	17,000	22,000	25,000	14,000

13	14	15	16	17	18
20,000	20,000	80,000	80,000	120,000	20,000

19	20	21	22	23	24
5,000,000	40,000	70,000	190,000	70,000	80,000

Worksheet 8

1	2	3	4	5	6	7
11,658	4,721	5,823	22,647	328,721	13,740	13,200

8	9	10	11	12	13	14
126,476	28,100	3,692	4,110	21,640	14,772	3,929

15	16	17	18	19	20	21
20,530	3,083	17,853	11,577	26,387	328,017	13,840

22	23	24	25	26	27
316,387	1,246,014	100,575	1,119,492	1,805,008	386,993

Worksheet 9

1	2	3	4	5	6
34,851	149,675	58,248	41,840	132,600	375,515

7	8	9	10	11	12
354,164	770,544	1,000,563	1,083,392	1,365,076	726,070

13	14	15
381,821	37,600	274,054

Worksheet 10

1	2	3	4	5	6	7
951	254	4,225	2,043	10,747	7,225	7,800

8	9	10	11	12	13	14
4,667	1,702	5,558	90	604	14,362	829

15	16	17	18	19	20	21
4,532	273	1,437	1,090	1,579	19,601	21,573

22	23	24	25	26	27
15,587	111,598	29,946	850,508	15,550,602	1,596

Worksheet 11

1	2	3	4	5	6	7	8
1,930	830	1,110	2,770	2,580	4,170	25,160	26,300

9	10	11	12	13	14	15
57,961	31,900	22,670	808	110,817	1,826	4,960

Worksheet 12

1	2	3	4	5	6	7	8
31,044	903	54,643	1,899	269,443	6,943	35,360	144,096

9	10	11	12	13	14	15
7,898	40,146	26,960	1,389,240	20,110	29,599	141,401

Worksheet 13

1	2	3	4	5	6	7	8	9	10	11	12	13	14	15
42	72	96	60	80	72	45	90	72	126	108	48	91	135	126

16	17	18	19	20	21	22	23	24	25	26	27	28
80	90	104	153	119	85	108	52	99	44	108	75	68

Worksheet 14

1	2	3	4	5	6	7	8	9	10	11	12	13	14	15
24	9	10	21	2	8	3	10	9	4	7	0	3	0	8

16	17	18	19	20	21	22	23	24	25	26	27	28
6	7	6	15	11	8	7	9	12	9	10	0	9

Worksheet 15

1	2	3
2 rows of 5 = 10 2 x 5 = 10	3 rows of 4 = 12 3 x 4 = 12	4 rows of 5 = 20 4 x 5 = 20

4	5	6
3 rows of 5 = 15 3 x 5 = 15	3 rows of 7 = 21 3 x 7 = 21	4 rows of 6 = 24 4 x 6 = 24

Worksheet 16

1	2	3	4	5
6 x 20 = 120	8 x 50 = 400	6 x 70 = 420	7 x 40 = 280	5 x 70 = 350

6	7	8	9	10
4 x 100 = 400	3 x 40 = 120	2 x 100 = 200	9 x 50 = 450	8 x 60 = 480

Worksheet 17

1	2	3
6 x 78 = 6 (70 + 8) = (6 x 70) + (6 x 8) = 420 + 48 = 468	9 x 27 = 9 (20 + 7) = (9 x 20) + (9 x 7) = 180 + 63 = 243	8 x 79 = 8 (70 + 9) = (8 x 70) + (8 x 9) = 560 + 72 = 632

126

Worksheet 18

1	2	3	4	5	6	7	8	9	10	11	12	13	14	15
54	64	200	130	60	252	204	117	370	468	512	207	568	144	284

16	17	18	19	20	21	22	23	24
584	384	576	440	540	152	105	300	588

Worksheet 19

1	2	3	4	5	6	7	8	9
1,944	1,278	2,888	3,360	4,680	3,072	1,494	2,292	2,313

10	11	12	13	14	15	16	17	18
3,528	1,512	2,196	6,858	1,512	6,055	5,492	1,782	1,825

19	20	21	22	23	24
1,024	2,184	716	1,996	1,536	2,947

Worksheet 20

1	2	3	4	5	6	7	8	9
792	968	1,350	1,027	1,296	1,287	1,577	1,513	6,156

10	11	12	13	14	15	16	17	18
4,819	1,007	551	4,680	552	5,175	3,630	1,350	864

19	20	21	22	23	24	25
1,064	975	816	1,184	1,274	2,772	1,848

Worksheet 21

1	2	3	4	5	6	7	8	9	10	11	12	13	14	15
3	11	6	6	6	3	16	5	12	8	10	7	10	13	6

16	17	18	19	20	21	22	23	24	25	26	27
10	9	12	9	7	11	8	11	9	8	6	7

Worksheet 22

1	2	3	4	5	6	7	8	9	10	11	12	13	14	15
11	12	17	22	9	6	18	10	10R2	34	37	34	16R1	9R6	12R5

16	17	18	19	20	21	22	23	24
21R2	9R5	14R1	5R3	16R2	1R1	8R5	21R3	13R2

Worksheet 23

1	2	3	4	5	6	7	8	9
217	179	161	168	111R4	256	53R1	28R2	97

10	11	12	13	14	15	16
17	26	52	139R2	25R1	17	448

Worksheet 24

1	2	3	4	5
1,2,3,4,6,8,12,16,24,48	1,3,17,51	1,19	1,3,5,15	1,2,3,5,6,15,30

6	7	8	9
1,5,13,65	1,2,3,5,6,10,15,18,30,45,90	1,7,11,77	1,2,4,5,10,20,25,50,100

10	11	12
1,7,49	1,2,3,6,9,18,27,54	1,3,13,39

Worksheet 25

1)

1	②	③	4	⑤
6	⑦	8	9	10
⑪	12	⑬	14	15
16	⑰	18	⑲	20
21	22	㉓	24	25

2)

1	2	3	④	5
⑥	7	⑧	⑨	⑩
11	⑫	13	⑭	⑮
⑯	17	⑱	19	⑳
㉑	㉒	23	㉔	㉕

128

Worksheet 26

1	2	3	4
13,16,19,22,25,28	27,37,47,57,67,77	0,5,10,15,20,25	0,6,18,30,42,54

5	6	7	8
21,30,39,48,57,66	21,23,25,27,29,31	2,12,22,32,42,52	10,25,35,45,55,65

9	10
20,33,45,57,69,71	52,57,62,67,72,77

Worksheet 27

1	2	3	4
28,32,36,40,44	60,65,70,75,80	90,120,150,180,210	42,84,126,168,252

5	6	7	8
1,3,4,5,6,7	1,3,5,7,9,10	40,50,60,70,80,90	33,39,45,51,57,63

9	10
12,18,24,27,30,33	2,3,4,5,7,9

Worksheet 28

1	2	3	4	5	6	7
Proper	Proper	Proper	Improper	Improper	Proper	Improper

8	9	10	11	12	13	14
Proper	Proper	Improper	B	D	D	A

Worksheet 29

1	2	3	4	5	6	7	8	9	10	11	12	13	14	15
2	5	10	7	25	12	50	60	80	4	3	6	B	D	D

Worksheet 30

1	2	3	4	5	6	7	8	9	10	11	12	13	14
$\frac{1}{2}$	$\frac{1}{2}$	$\frac{1}{3}$	$\frac{1}{3}$	$\frac{1}{3}$	$\frac{1}{5}$	$\frac{1}{4}$	$\frac{1}{3}$	$\frac{2}{3}$	$\frac{3}{4}$	$\frac{1}{7}$	$\frac{1}{5}$	$\frac{1}{4}$	$\frac{2}{5}$

Worksheet 31

1	2	3	4	5	6	7	8	9	10	11	12	13	14	15
<	>	<	<	>	>	>	>	<	<	>	=	>	=	=

16	17	18
D	A	A

Worksheet 32

1	2	3	4	5
$\frac{1}{4} < \frac{2}{4} < \frac{3}{4}$	$\frac{2}{9} < \frac{3}{9} < \frac{4}{9}$	$\frac{1}{4} < \frac{3}{8} < \frac{5}{8}$	$\frac{3}{5} < \frac{2}{3} < \frac{5}{10}$	$\frac{1}{5} < \frac{1}{4} < \frac{1}{3}$

6	7	8	9
$\frac{2}{3} < \frac{7}{10} < \frac{4}{5}$	$\frac{2}{9} < \frac{3}{9} < \frac{4}{9}$	$\frac{7}{2} < \frac{9}{2} < \frac{11}{2}$	$\frac{2}{7} < \frac{3}{5} < \frac{3}{2}$

Worksheet 33

1	2	3	4	5	6	7	8	9	10	11	12	13	14	15
$5\frac{1}{3}$	$1\frac{7}{10}$	$\frac{15}{19}$	$\frac{3}{4}$	$1\frac{1}{3}$	$2\frac{5}{7}$	$3\frac{2}{11}$	$\frac{9}{10}$	$1\frac{10}{17}$	$\frac{1}{3}$	$\frac{2}{3}$	$\frac{4}{19}$	$\frac{9}{14}$	$\frac{11}{20}$	$3\frac{16}{17}$

16	17	18	19	20	21
3	6	2	3	$6\frac{2}{5}$	7

Worksheet 34

1	2	3	4	5	6	7	8	9	10	11	12	13	14	15
$5\frac{2}{3}$	$\frac{2}{3}$	$1\frac{13}{19}$	2	1	$\frac{6}{7}$	$\frac{4}{11}$	$\frac{1}{10}$	$2\frac{13}{17}$	$1\frac{4}{15}$	$\frac{4}{5}$	$3\frac{5}{19}$	$\frac{1}{14}$	$\frac{11}{10}$	1

16	17	18	19	20	21
2	$\frac{9}{10}$	$\frac{1}{3}$	1	2	3

Worksheet 35

1	2	3	4	5	6	7	8	9	10	11	12	13	14	15
$2\frac{1}{2}$	$5\frac{2}{5}$	$7\frac{1}{3}$	$10\frac{2}{5}$	$2\frac{1}{4}$	$8\frac{4}{5}$	$4\frac{6}{7}$	5	$12\frac{4}{5}$	$13\frac{1}{2}$	$12\frac{2}{3}$	$23\frac{1}{2}$	$10\frac{2}{7}$	24	35

16
$13\frac{1}{4}$

Worksheet 36

1	2	3	4	5	6	7	8	9	10	11	12	13	14	15
$\frac{1}{3}$	4	$4\frac{1}{2}$	$4\frac{2}{5}$	2	1	$3\frac{8}{9}$	3	4	1	5	4	3	10	$6\frac{4}{5}$

16
$1\frac{2}{3}$

Worksheet 37

1	2	3	4	5	6	7	8	9	10	11	12	13	14	15
$\frac{5}{6}$	$\frac{7}{60}$	$\frac{5}{36}$	$\frac{1}{3}$	$\frac{10}{27}$	$\frac{1}{24}$	$\frac{3}{4}$	$\frac{3}{8}$	5	$\frac{3}{10}$	4	$\frac{1}{40}$	$\frac{1}{2}$	$\frac{1}{28}$	2

16	17	18	19	20	21
$\frac{5}{8}$	$1\frac{2}{3}$	$\frac{7}{10}$	$2\frac{2}{3}$	$3\frac{1}{2}$	$10\frac{3}{8}$

Worksheet 38

1	2	3	4	5	6	7	8	9	10	11	12	13	14	15
6	$\frac{2}{5}$	$\frac{1}{2}$	$2\frac{3}{5}$	$\frac{5}{16}$	$6\frac{1}{9}$	6	$\frac{6}{7}$	3	1	9	1	$\frac{12}{35}$	$8\frac{2}{3}$	$3\frac{3}{5}$

16
$3\frac{3}{8}$

Worksheet 39

Worksheet 40

1)

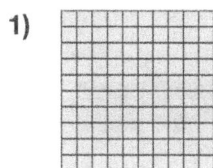

$\boxed{1}$

2)

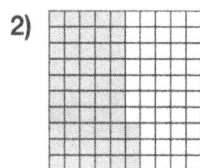

$\boxed{0.54}$

3)

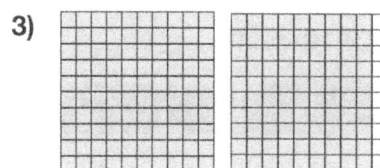

$\boxed{1.9}$

4)

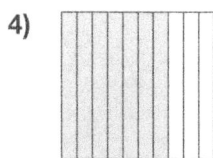

$\boxed{0.7}$

5)

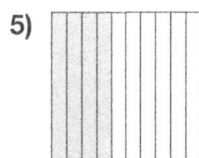

$\boxed{0.4}$

6)

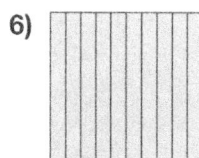

$\boxed{1}$

7)

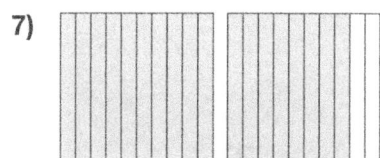

$\boxed{1.8}$

8)

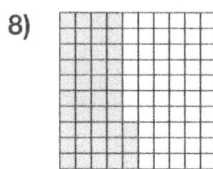

$\boxed{0.43}$

9)

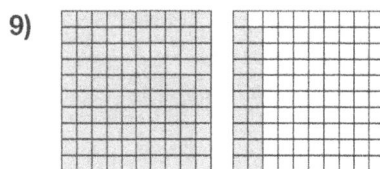

$\boxed{\text{1 and 19 hundredths}}$

10)

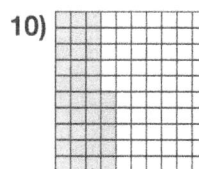

$\boxed{\text{35 hundredths}}$

11)

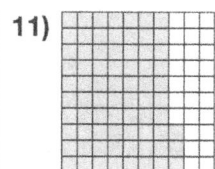

$\boxed{0,73}$

12)

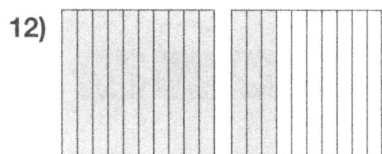

$\boxed{1.3}$

13)

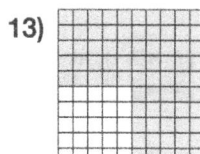

$\boxed{0.75}$

14)

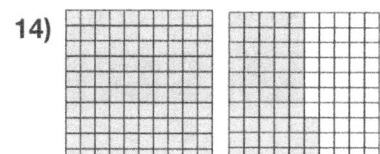

$\boxed{1.53}$

132

Worksheet 41

1	2	3	4	5	6	7	8	9	10	11	12	13	14	15
0.4	0.8	1.1	0.5	0.7	3.2	0.6	1	4.1	$\frac{3}{10}$	$\frac{4}{10}$	$\frac{7}{10}$	$\frac{1}{2}$	$\frac{4}{4}$	$\frac{1}{5}$

16	17	18	19	20	21	22	23	24	25	26	27	28	29	30
$\frac{9}{10}$	$\frac{3}{5}$	$\frac{11}{10}$	0.93	0.12	0.88	0.90	0.35	0.77	$\frac{47}{100}$	$\frac{71}{100}$	$\frac{19}{100}$	$\frac{61}{100}$	$\frac{46}{100}$	$\frac{118}{100}$

Worksheet 42

1	2	3	4	5	6	7	8	9	10	11	12	13	14
>	=	>	<	<	<	>	>	>	>	>	>	<	=

Worksheet 43

1	2	3
10,000 20,000 30,000 40,000 50,000	5,000 10,000 15,000 20,000 25,000	500 1,000 1,500 2,000 2,500

4	5	6
20 40 60 80 100	1,000 2,000 3,000 4,000 5,000	1,000 2,000 3,000 4,000 5,000

Worksheet 44

1	2	3
4,8,12,16,20	12,24,36,48,60	16,32,48,64,80

4	5	6
9,18,27,36,45	80,160,240,320,400	10,000 20,000 30,000 40,000 50,000

Worksheet 45

1	2	3	4	5	6	7	8	9	10	11	12	13	14	15
900	1,200	1,080	240	5	15	720	84	50	5,760	1	264	35	208	10

16	17	18	19	20
336	42	72	7,200	1,095

Worksheet 46

1	2	3	4	5	6
Obtuse	Straight	Acute	Right	Acute	Obtuse

7	8	9	10	11	12
Right	Acute	Obtuse	Acute	Obtuse	Right

Worksheet 47

1	2	3	4	5	6	7	8	9
85	60	108	57	45	150	55	61	63

Worksheet 48

1	2	3	4	5
Equilateral	Isosceles	Scalene	Equilateral	Acute

6	7	8	9
Obtuse	Obtuse Isosceles	Acute Isosceles	Right Isosceles

Worksheet 49

Grouping	Sides	Angels	Parallel Sides
Rectangle	4 sides	4 right angles	Opposite sides are parallel
Square	4 sides	4 right angles	Opposite sides are parallel
Trapezoid	4 sides	4 diff. angels	Only one pair of sides is parallel
Rhombus	4 sides	4 angels	Opposite sides are parallel
Parallelogram	4 sides	4 angels	Opposite sides are parallel
Kite	4 sides	4 angels	No parallel sides

Worksheet 50

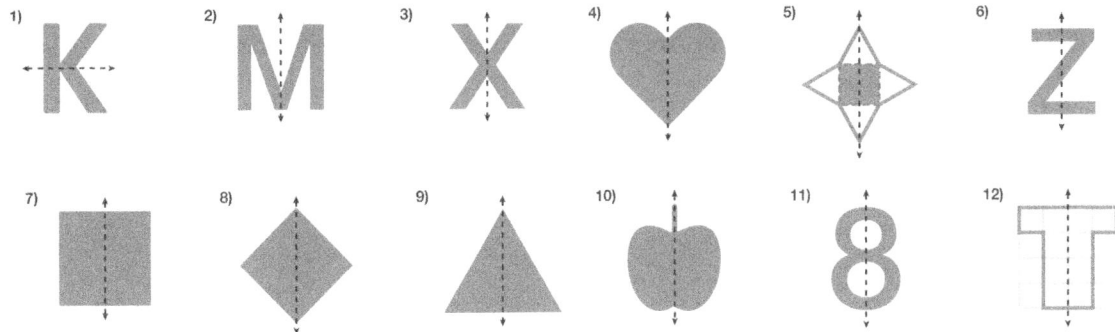

Worksheet 51

1	2	3	4	5	6	7	8	9
18 m	44 in.	22 yards	18 ft	24 m	24 ft	32 in.	26 cm	30 cm

Worksheet 52

1	2	3	4	5	6
24 cm	12 cm	28 cm	19 cm	32 cm	60 cm

7	8	9	10	11	12
12 units	15 units	25 units	24 m	20 cm	24 ft

Worksheet 53

1	2	3	4	5	6
12 Square u.	15 Square u.	25 Square u.	36 cm^2	9 cm^2	49 cm^2

7	8	9	10	11	12
20 Square u.	25 Square u.	36 Square u.	15 Square u.	12 Square u.	24 Square u.

Worksheet 54

1	2	3	4	5
Area: 70cm^2 Perimeter: 34cm	Area: 72m^2 Perimeter: 36m	Area: 500ft^2 Perimeter: 112ft	Area: 208cm^2 Perimeter: 68m	Area: 95m^2 Perimeter: 42m

Worksheet 55

1) Coordinates	Point
(4, 8)	A
(-6, 6)	B
(3, 3)	C
(4, 0)	D
(3, -6)	E
(0, -8)	F
(-8, -5)	G

2	3	4
D	B	D

Mixed Review Test 1

1	2	3	4	5	6	7	8	9	10	11	12	13	14	15
D	A	C	A	A	B	A	A	A	A	C	B	B	A	A

16	17	18	19	20	21	22	23	24
D	A	B	A	A	B	A	B	B

Mixed Review Test 2

1	2	3	4	5	6	7	8	9	10	11	12	13	14	15
B	C	B	B	A	A	B	A	A	A	A	C	C	C	B

16	17	18	19	20	21	22	23	24
C	A	C	B	B	B	A	A	A

Mixed Review Test 3

1	2	3	4	5	6	7	8	9	10	11	12	13	14	15
C	B	B	B	A	A	B	A	A	A	A	C	A	C	A

16	17	18	19	20	21	22	23	24	25	26	27	28	29	30
A	A	A	B	B	A	A	D	A	C	A	D	A	A	A

31	32	33	34	35	36
A	A	A	A	B	D

Mixed Review Test 4

1	2	3	4	5	6	7	8	9	10	11	12	13	14	15
C	C	C	B	C	C	C	D	C	A	D	C	C	D	B

16	17	18	19	20	21	22	23	24
B	D	B	B	B	B	D	B	D

Mixed Review Test 5

1	2	3	4	5	6	7	8	9	10	11	12	13	14	15
A	A	C	C	B	D	A	B	B	B	A	B	A	B	B

16	17	18	19	20	21	22	23	24
B	A	C	A	B	A	B	B	B

Mixed Review Test 6

1	2	3	4	5	6	7	8	9	10	11	12	13	14	15
B	C	B	A	A	B	A	A	A	B	A	C	A	A	D

16	17	18	19	20	21	22	23	24
A	A	B	B	A	C	C	C	A

Mixed Review Test 7

1	2	3	4	5	6	7	8	9	10	11	12	13	14	15
C	A	C	A	B	A	B	B	C	A	D	B	C	B	B

16	17	18	19	20	21	22	23	24
A	B	A	C	A	C	D	D	C

Mixed Review Test 8

1	2	3	4	5	6	7	8	9	10	11	12	13	14	15
B	A	C	C	C	C	A	C	D	C	D	A	A	D	B

16	17	18
A	D	C

Mixed Review Test 9

1	2	3	4	5	6	7	8	9	10	11	12	13	14	15
C	D	C	D	C	C	C	B	C	D	D	D	D	C	D

16	17	18	19	20	21	22	23	24
D	C	C	C	B	D	C	D	B

Mixed Review Test 10

1	2	3	4	5	6	7	8	9	10	11	12	13	14	15
B	A	A	B	B	A	C	C	A	B	A	B	A	B	D

16	17	18	19	20	21	22	23	24	25	26	27	28	29	30
A	B	A	B	A	D	B	A	D	A	C	B	A	A	B

31	32	33	34
B	A	D	B

Post-Test

1	2	3	4	5	6	7	8	9	10	11	12	13	14	15
D	C	C	D	A	D	D	B	D	C	C	A	A	D	B

16	17	18	19	20	21	22	23	24	25	26	27	28	29	30
B	D	B	B	D	C	D	B	C	C	A	B	D	D	A

31	32	33	34	35	36	37	38	39	40	41	42	43	44	45
B	B	D	C	C	C	D	C	C	C	C	C	B	B	D

46	47	48	49	50	51	52	53
B	A	B	A	A	C	C	C

NOTE

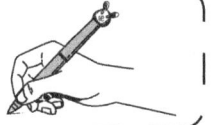

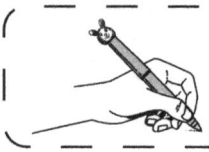

NOTE

NOTE

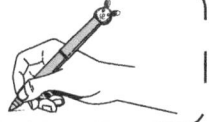

Made in the USA
Las Vegas, NV
11 March 2025

19421966R00083